THE LEARNED LADIES

WITHDRAWN

ALSO BY RICHARD WILBUR

The Beautiful Changes and Other Poems

Ceremony and Other Poems

A Bestiary (editor, with Alexander Calder)

Molière's *The Misanthrope* (translator)

Things of This World

Poems 1943–1958

Candide (with Lillian Hellman)

Poe: Complete Poems (editor)

Advice to a Prophet and Other Poems

Molière's *Tartuffe* (translator)

The Poems of Richard Wilbur

Loudmouse (for children)

Shakespeare: Poems (co-editor, with Alfred Harbage)

Walking to Sleep: New Poems and Translations

Molière's *The School for Wives* (translator)

Opposites (for children and others)

The Mind-Reader: New Poems

Responses: Prose Pieces: 1953–1976

DRAWINGS BY ENRICO ARNO

JEAN BAPTISTE POQUELIN DE MOLIÈRE

The Learned Ladies

COMEDY IN FIVE ACTS, 1672

TRANSLATED INTO ENGLISH VERSE BY

RICHARD WILBUR

HARCOURT BRACE JOVANOVICH

NEW YORK AND LONDON

Printed in the United States of America

CAUTION: Professionals and amateurs are hereby warned that *The Learned Ladies* is subject to a royalty. It is fully protected under the copyright laws of the United States of America, and of all countries covered by the International Copyright Union (including the Dominion of Canada and the rest of the British Commonwealth), and of all countries covered by the Universal Copyright Convention and the Pan-American Copyright Convention, and of all countries with which the United States has reciprocal copyright relations. All rights, including professional, amateur, motion picture, recitation, lecturing, public reading, radio broadcasting, television and the rights of translation into foreign languages, are strictly reserved. Particular emphasis is laid on the question of readings, permission for which must be secured from the author's agent in writing. All inquiries (except for amateur rights) should be addressed to Gilbert Parker, Curtis Brown, Ltd., 575 Madison Avenue, New York, N.Y. 10022.

The amateur acting rights of *The Learned Ladies* are controlled exclusively by the Dramatists Play Service, Inc., 440 Park Avenue South, New York, N.Y. 10016. No amateur performance of the play may be given without obtaining in advance the written permission of the Dramatists Play Service, Inc., and paying the requisite fee.

Library of Congress Cataloging in Publication Data

Molière, Jean Baptiste Poquelin, 1622–1673.
The learned ladies.

Translation of Les Femmes savantes.
I. Wilbur, Richard, 1921–   II. Title.
PQ1833.A475   1978   842'.4   77-85199
ISBN 0-15-149480-0
ISBN 0-15-649501-5 pbk.

A B C D E F G H I J

For Gilbert Parker

INTRODUCTION

The Learned Ladies resembles *Tartuffe* in that it is the drama of a bourgeois household which has lost its harmony and balance through some recent change. In the case of *Tartuffe*, what has changed is that the head of the house, Orgon, who was formerly a sound and solid man, has succumbed to a sort of specious and menopausal religious frenzy. The whole action of the play follows from this aberration of Orgon's, and the whole familial fabric of affections and responsibilities is shaken before the action is over. In *The Learned Ladies* it is once more—though less obviously—the head of the house to whom the disruption of normal relationships may be traced. Chrysale is a soft, comfort-loving person who speaks too often of "my collars" and "my roast of beef." He considers himself peace-loving and gentle, and his daughter Henriette is so kind as to describe his weakness as good nature; but in fact he is an ineffectual man, given to dreaming of his youth, who has always avoided the unpleasantness of exercising his authority as husband and father. The power vacuum thus created has been fully occupied, not long before the play begins, by Chrysale's wilful wife, Philaminte.

It was an unnatural thing, in the view of Molière's audience, for a wife to assume the husband's dominant role, and this is plainly illustrated by the fact that, in early productions of *Les femmes savantes*, the part of Philaminte was played by a male actor. In usurping the headship of the household, Philaminte has become an unsexed woman or the caricature of a man: instead of quiet authority, she has a vain and impatient coerciveness, and her domestic rule amounts to a reign of terror. Her ambition, and a measure of intelligence, lead her to become a bluestocking and, in emulation of certain great ladies, to turn her house into an academy and salon. She enlists in this program her unmarried sister-in-law, Bélise, and her elder daughter, Armande. The spirited and sensible younger daughter, Henriette, declines to be recruited.

In *Les précieuses ridicules* (1659), Molière had made farcical fun of middle-class young women who aspired to salon life, with its refinements of speech and manner, its witticisms, its "spiritual" gallantries, its madrigals and *bouts-rimés*. As the century grew older, salon habitués became concerned with science and philosophy as well, so that Molière's Learned Ladies of 1672 keep a telescope in the attic and make references to Descartes and Epicurus. The atmosphere, *chez* Philaminte, is above all Platonic. Mind and soul are exalted, the body is scorned, and marriage is viewed with contempt. This ambiance is emotionally convenient for Bélise, who adopts the fantasy that all men are secretly and ethereally in love with her, and who also appeases her balked maternal instinct by schooling the servants in elementary grammar and science. For Armande, membership in her mother's "academy" is a less comfortable fate. Following Philaminte's example, she proclaims a pure devotion to spirit and intellect, and a horror of material and bodily things; but in fact she can neither satisfy herself with intellectual activity nor detach herself from the flesh. She would be a touching figure, as many are who suffer from imperfect idealism, were it not for her pretentiousness and for her jealous spite toward those who enjoy what she has renounced.

The abdication of Chrysale, in other words, has precipitated an abnormal situation in which all of the main characters suffer deformity or strain. Bélise is pacified by her chimeras, but at the cost of a complete divorce from the real feelings of others: when Henriette's suitor, Clitandre, turns to her for help in the play's fourth scene, he might as well be addressing a dead woman. Armande, saddled with an aspiration which is too much for her, is condemned to imposture and envy. Philaminte's bullying insistence on creating an intellectual environment arises not from a true thirst for knowledge but from a desire for personal glory, as well as a rancorous wish (which she shares with Armande) to show men that

> *women may be learnèd if they please,*
> *And found, like men, their own academies.*

Because of the ruthless egoism of her project, and its spirit of revenge, Philaminte suppresses in herself the magnanimity which truly belongs to her nature, and which flashes out briefly in the final scene of the play. Her vanity may also be blamed for the blindness with which she admires the egregious pedant Trissotin, and the heartlessness with which she presses Henriette to marry him against her wishes.

And what of Henriette? Is she, as one French critic has said, a "hateful girl" given to false humility, cutting ironies, and banal conceptions of life? Certainly not. I am of Arthur Tilley's opinion, that "her simplicity, her directness, and above all, her sense of humor, make her the most delightful of Molière's young women." She is far more intelligent and witty than her highfalutin sister, Armande; she is filial without being spiritless; independent without being rebellious; admirable in accepting the fact that she is her lover's second choice; noble in her readiness to release him from what temporarily seems a bad bargain. To find any of her speeches abrasive is to forget her embattled and near-desperate position as a younger daughter under pressure from three variously demented women. We must judge her as we would a noncollaborative citizen of some occupied country. Defending herself against Armande, she banters and teases; with her mother, she sometimes plays dumb or dull; to Clitandre, she gives blunt and practical strategic advice; in her bold confrontation with Trissotin, she proves a cunning debater, and concludes with an understandable asperity. In all of this, she shows her resourcefulness and pluck, but each tactic necessarily entails a temporary distortion of her nature in reaction to circumstances. Of Clitandre, too, it may be supposed that the situation exaggerates some of his attitudes, and turns him into more of a ranter than he would usually be.

The Learned Ladies comes as close to being a satiric play as does anything in Molière's *oeuvre*; yet here as everywhere he subordinates satire to the comic spirit, which is less interested in excoriating human error than in affirming the fullness of life. As always in Molière, there lies in the background of the play a clear and actual France: it is an absolute monarchy with a Catholic culture and a powerful Church; it is characterized by strong class distinctions; in it, all social or familial roles, such as the father's ruling function in any household, are plain matters of natural law; it is a highly centralized state, and life at court or in Paris is very different from life in the provinces. Other basic aspects of Molière's France might be cited; suffice it, however, to add that behind this particular play (as behind *The Misanthrope*) there also lies the Paris of social and literary cliques and

[*Introduction*]

salons, an élite world which considered itself more elegant than the court. Our understanding of the characters in *The Learned Ladies* is partially shaped by an awareness of the real France beyond them: we note, for instance, that for the upper-middle-class Philaminte the conducting of a salon is a form of social climbing, and that it gratifies her to hear Trissotin recite under her roof a sonnet which has lately pleased "a certain princess." The life of the characters does *not*, however, consist in the satiric indication of real persons belonging to the salon world of Paris; their vitality and depth result, as I have been trying to suggest, from their intense interplay with each other, and from the way in which an unbalanced family situation has warped, divided, or challenged their personalities. We look *at* and *into* Philaminte or Armande, not *through* them.

To this rule there are a couple of apparent exceptions. The name of Philaminte's salon guest Trissotin was, for the seventeenth-century ear, inevitably suggestive of Molière's contemporary Charles Cotin. A member of the French Academy and a frequenter of the most brilliant salons, the Abbé Cotin was a prolific writer of occasional verse, who had more than once satirically attacked Molière and his friend Boileau. Molière avenged himself by naming an unattractive character Trissotin ("thrice-a-fool"), and also by having that character recite as his own work two vulnerably arch poems of Cotin's composition. In Vadius, with whom Trissotin has a literary spat in Act III, audiences easily recognized a reference to the distinguished scholar Gilles Ménage, who made verses in French, Italian, Latin, and Greek, and had once, by several accounts, quarreled with Cotin over the merits of one of the latter's poems. Vadius and Trissotin resemble Ménage and Cotin in the above respects, and one might add that Ménage was well known for the peremptoriness of his aesthetic judgments, and Cotin for being vain of his literary productions. But there the resemblances stop. When *Les femmes savantes* was first acted, Cotin was a sixty-eight-year-old man in holy orders, and could not possibly be confused with the fortune-hunting Trissotin of Act V. No more was Vadius intended as a true portrait of Ménage. Though French audiences of 1672 could enjoy Molière's incidental thrusts as we cannot, the figures of Trissotin and Vadius were finally for them, as for us, two fictional sketches of salon wits. Satire, then, is a secondary and local effect in this play, and the two wits, though less complex than certain other characters, share the same fictional world with them, and serve the same plot and theme.

Plot, in Molière, is best not taken too hard. We should not hold our breaths, toward the close of *Tartuffe*, over the danger that Orgon will lose his property; Molière was not, after all, writing bourgeois melodrama. And neither *The School for Wives* nor *The Learned Ladies* should make us bite our nails for fear that Agnès or Henriette will be forced to marry the wrong man. The use of plot in Molière is, as W. G. Moore has said, "to present an abstract issue in concrete pictures"; the plot is there to shuffle the characters around, providing us with all the confrontations and revelations that are necessary to depict a comic deformity and to define it by contrast to saner behaviors. From this transpires the play's question or theme—which is, in the case of *The Learned Ladies*, the right relation of art and learning to everyday life.

Every major figure in the play, whether male or female, somehow embodies that theme, and the men have their fair share of odiousness and folly. Chrysale, expressing an attitude that many of his original audience would have endorsed, holds that women's "only study and philosophy" should be the rearing of children, the training of servants, the keeping of household accounts, and the making of trousseaus. Nor is he more intellectually ambitious for himself: while there may be nothing scandalous about his indifference to the revolutions of Saturn, he is thoroughly philistine in his scorn of all books save the heavy Plutarch in which he presses his collars. Chrysale's brother, Ariste, is actually more of a catalyst than a character, but one or two of his speeches share Chrysale's distaste for pedantry and for "besotted" intellectuality in women; and the kitchen maid, Martine, vehemently supports her master's aversion to having a bookworm for a son-in-law. None of these persons, of course, speaks for Molière: Ariste's remarks are conditioned by his role as Clitandre's advocate; Chrysale is self-centered and hidebound, and appeals to us only through his wholesome sympathy with young love; Martine has a certain instinctual wisdom, but can scarcely be trusted to appreciate the value that education might have for her betters. And yet we side with this faction, and second what is valid in their speeches, because the "learned ladies" are so

[*Introduction*]

ill-motivated and their heroes—Trissotin and Vadius—so appalling. Philaminte, Bélise, and Armande lack, as I have said, any real vocation for the life of the mind, and Act III demonstrates this in numerous ways. By their continual interruption of Trissotin's verses, the ladies show that they have small interest in poetry proper; by their fatuous praise of Trissotin's verses, they show that they have no taste. The "learning" they display is skimpy and ludicrous, and their dreams of an academy have less to do with knowledge than with self-assertion and celebrity. Finally, the scenes with Trissotin and Vadius are so full of coquetry, so charged with repressed sexuality, as to prove the ladies unfitted to be vestals of science and of the spirit. All this being the case, Philaminte and her associates represent a false and fruitless intellectual pretension which entails neglect of all the normal self-realizations and responsibilities of bourgeois women. As for Trissotin's relation to the theme of this play, he is someone for whom learning, or, rather, a literary career, has become the whole of life. Regarding the poems which he dedicates to "Irises and Phyllises," he assures Henriette that

My mind speaks in those verses, not my heart.

But in fact this desiccated man has no heart, and for all his mixing in society, he is perfectly antisocial in the sense of being perfectly selfish; all of his attentions and flatteries to Philaminte's circle, all of his intrigues for dowry or pension, are for the benefit of a self which consists wholly of literary vanity and the pursuit of reputation. Literature and thought, for such a man, are unreal because unrelated to human feeling; in consequence, his life is vicious and his verse is dead.

The healthiest attitudes toward the play's theme are embodied in, and expressed by, Clitandre and Henriette. In respect of two repeated topics, spirituality and language, they represent an agreeable median position. Philaminte and Armande urge a life of pure intellect, and Bélise will have nothing to do with "extended substance"; Chrysale, at the other extreme, identifies himself with his body (*mon corps est moi-même*); but in Act IV, Scene 2, Clitandre firmly tells Armande that he has "both a body and a spirit," and Henriette has already proven the same of herself in the first scene of the play. In regard to language, we have at one extreme the pungent, direct, but limited and ungrammatical speech of Martine; at the other, we have the stifling or prissy rules of the proposed academy, the substanceless flatteries and phrase-making of Trissotin and Vadius, and the absolute dissociation of style and function in Philaminte's proposal that a French marriage contract express the dowry "in talent and drachma," and be dated in "ides and calends." (Since Philaminte twice upbraids the notary for his barbaric style, it is amusing that she is here proposing the use of literal barbarisms.) Though Henriette's speech is at times strategically flat, and though Clitandre, when aroused, can rattle on for thirty lines like Hotspur, their discourse is, on the whole, straightforward, pithy, sprightly, and graceful, and amounts to the best employment of language in the play. The virtues of Clitandre and Henriette are not all to be discovered in some middle ground, however: for instance, despite all the high-minded talk of others, it is they who, in the final scene, represent the extreme of active unselfishness in *Les femmes savantes*.

It is possible to exaggerate the play's anti-intellectualism. One should remember that the action takes place not in the university, the church, a great salon, or the manor house of Madame de Sévigné, but in an upper-bourgeois milieu, where an ill-founded pursuit of the semblance of culture can pervert all of the norms of life. Molière does not deny that there may be truly learned men and women, or true literati like Boileau, and he has Clitandre speak of persons of genuine wit and brain who are not unwelcome at the court. If the pseudo-intellectuality of the "learned ladies" were not so flamboyant, and Clitandre and Henriette so occupied with resisting it, one would more readily notice that the young lovers are literate people who read poetry (Trissotin's, for example) and judge it with some accuracy. Clitandre, it should be observed, is not unfamiliar with the scholarship of Rasius and Baldus, and is capable of criticizing the Platonic separation of body and soul. He and Henriette are in fact witty, intelligent, tasteful, and independent-minded; yet they do not feel that the cultivation of the mind should estrange one from life's basic fulfillments and duties. Neither, clearly, does Molière.

Clitandre's assertion that "A woman should know something . . . / Of every subject" was a quite liberal sentiment for its day, but we will not now recognize it as such unless *The Learned Ladies* is read (or mounted) quite strictly "in period."

[Introduction]

Molière is a timeless author in the sense that his art, owing to its clarity and its concern with human fundamentals, is not only readily enjoyed by readers and audiences three centuries after his death, but is often, I think, taken pretty much as it was meant to be taken. This freshness of Molière, his present accessibility, has lately misled some theatrical companies into detaching his art from its temporal background, and giving it the kind of "updating" which involves absurd anachronisms and the loss of meaning through the loss of a credible social frame. Not long ago, I saw a production that aimed to make *Tartuffe* "relevant" by dressing the title character in the sheets and beads of a guru, and having the action take place around a family swimming pool in California. The attempt at topicality was, of course, doomed from the start: it was young people who, in the latter 1960's, were succumbing to the influence of gurus, whereas in Molière's play that is not the situation at all: the children, Damis and Mariane, regard Tartuffe as a fraud, and it is their middle-aged father who is taken in. Not only did the production not mesh with current events, as the director had hoped it would seem to do; it was also miserably confusing, amongst other things, to hear a guru uttering Tartuffe's speeches, which are full of Christian scriptural and liturgical echoes, as well as seventeenth-century Jesuit terminology. More recently, a Boston company based a regrettable "modern-dress" production of *The Misanthrope* on the supposition that Alceste's demand for frankness in social intercourse resembles the demand, lately made by our youth culture, that one "tell it like it is." As a result, the play began with Alceste's entering a twentieth-century American living room in hippie attire, a ten-speed bicycle under his arm. The reader will imagine how implausibly such a figure inhabited the world of the text, where people are addressed as Sir and Madam, where duelling is a serious matter, and where continual reference is made to viscounts, marquesses, and the court of Versailles. I hope that no presenter of this new translation will wish, by means of contemporary costume and set, to attempt a violent conflation of Molière's drama with the current women's movement. And I hope that all readers of this text will envision it in a just historical perspective: Clitandre's liberalism, Henriette's attractively balanced nature, the grotesqueness of the bluestockings, and every nuance of this excellent comedy will then be there to be seen.

Sincere thanks are owed to my colleague Morton Briggs, who urged me to undertake this translation and was so kind as to read it over. I must also thank my wife, and Sonja and William Jay Smith, for their goodness in criticizing both the text and these remarks.

R. W.

Cummington, Massachusetts
May, 1977

THE LEARNED LADIES

CHARACTERS

CHRYSALE, a well-to-do bourgeois

PHILAMINTE, Chrysale's wife

ARMANDE and ⎱ daughters of Chrysale
HENRIETTE ⎰ and Philaminte

ARISTE, Chrysale's brother

BÉLISE, Chrysale's sister

CLITANDRE, Henriette's suitor

TRISSOTIN, a wit

VADIUS, a scholar

MARTINE, kitchen-maid

LÉPINE, a servant

JULIEN, valet to Vadius

A NOTARY

The scene: Chrysale's house in Paris

SCENE ONE

ARMANDE

What, Sister! Are you truly of a mind
To leave your precious maidenhood behind,
And give yourself in marriage to a man?
Can you be harboring such a vulgar plan?

HENRIETTE

Yes, Sister.

ARMANDE

           Yes, you say! When have I heard
So odious and sickening a word?

HENRIETTE

Why does the thought of marriage so repel you?

ARMANDE

Fie, fie! For shame!

HENRIETTE

       But what—

7

ARMANDE

For shame, I tell you!
Can you deny what sordid scenes are brought
To the mind's eye by that distasteful thought,
What coarse, degrading images arise,
What shocking things it makes one visualize?
Do you not shudder, Sister, and grow pale
At what this thought you're thinking would entail?

HENRIETTE

It would entail, as I conceive it, one
Husband, some children, and a house to run;
In all of which, it may as well be said,
I find no cause for loathing or for dread.

ARMANDE

Alas! Such bondage truly appeals to you?

HENRIETTE

At my young age, what better could I do
Than join myself in wedded harmony
To one I love, and who in turn loves me,
And through the deepening bond of man and wife
Enjoy a blameless and contented life?
Does such a union offer no attractions?

ARMANDE

Oh dear, you crave such squalid satisfactions!
How can you choose to play a petty role,
Dull and domestic, and content your soul
With joys no loftier than keeping house
And raising brats, and pampering a spouse?

Let common natures, vulgarly inclined,
Concern themselves with trifles of that kind.
Aspire to nobler objects, seek to attain
To keener joys upon a higher plane,
And, scorning gross material things as naught,
Devote yourself, as we have done, to thought.
We have a mother to whom all pay honor
For erudition; model yourself upon her;
Yes, prove yourself her daughter, as I have done,
Join in the quest for truth that she's begun,
And learn how love of study can impart
A sweet enlargement to the mind and heart.
Why marry, and be the slave of him you wed?
Be married to philosophy instead,
Which lifts us up above mankind, and gives
All power to reason's pure imperatives,
Thus rendering our bestial natures tame
And mastering those lusts which lead to shame.
A love of reason, a passion for the truth,
Should quite suffice one's heart in age or youth,
And I am moved to pity when I note
On what low objects certain women dote.

HENRIETTE

But Heaven, in its wise omnipotence,
Endows us all with differing gifts and bents,
And all souls are not fashioned, I'm afraid,
Of the stuff of which philosophers are made.
If yours was born for soaring to the heights
Of learning, and for speculative flights,
My own weak spirit, Sister, has from birth
Clung to the homelier pleasures of the earth.
Let's not oppose what Heaven has decreed,
But simply follow where our instincts lead.
You, through the towering genius you possess,
Shall dwell in philosophic loftiness,

While my prosaic nature, here below,
Shall taste such joys as marriage can bestow.
Thus, though our lives contrast with one another,
We each shall emulate our worthy mother—
You, in your quest for rational excellence,
I, in the less refined delights of sense;
You, in conceptions lofty and ethereal,
I, in conceptions rather more material.

ARMANDE

Sister, the person whom one emulates
Ought to be followed for her finer traits.
If someone's worthy to be copied, it's
Not for the way in which she coughs and spits.

HENRIETTE

You and your intellect would not be here
If Mother's traits had all been fine, my dear,
And it's most fortunate for you that she
Was not wed solely to philosophy.
Relent, and tolerate in me, I pray,
That urge through which you saw the light of day,
And do not bid me be like you, and scorn
The hopes of some small scholar to be born.

ARMANDE

Your mind, I see, is stupidly contrary,
And won't give up its stubborn wish to marry.
But tell me, do, of this intended match:
Surely it's not Clitandre you aim to catch?

HENRIETTE

Why not? Of what defects could one accuse him?
Would I be vulgar if I were to choose him?

[*Act One* · *Scene One*]

ARMANDE

No. But I don't think much of your design
To lure away a devotee of mine;
Clitandre, as the world well knows, has sighed
And yearned for me, and sought me as his bride.

HENRIETTE

Yes; but such sighs, arising as they do
From base affections, are as naught to you;
Marriage is something you have risen above,
And fair philosophy has all your love.
Since, then, Clitandre isn't necessary
To your well-being, may he and I not marry?

ARMANDE

Though reason bids us shun the baits of sense,
We still may take delight in compliments;
We may refuse a man, yet be desirous
That still he pay us homage, and admire us.

HENRIETTE

I never sought to make him discontinue
His worship of the noble soul that's in you;
But once you had refused him, I felt free
To take the love which he then offered me.

ARMANDE

When a rejected suitor, full of spite,
Claims to adore you, can you trust him quite?
Do you really think he loves you? Are you persuaded
That his intense desire for me has faded?

HENRIETTE

Yes, Sister, I believe it; he's told me so.

ARMANDE

Sister, you're gullible; as you should know,
His talk of leaving me and loving you
Is self-deceptive bluster, and quite untrue.

HENRIETTE

Perhaps; however, Sister, if you'd care
To learn with me the facts of this affair,
I see Clitandre coming; I'm sure, my dear,
That if we ask, he'll make his feelings clear.

SCENE TWO

CLITANDRE, ARMANDE, HENRIETTE

HENRIETTE

My sister has me in uncertainties
As to your heart's affections. If you please,
Clitandre, tell us where your feelings lie,
And which of us may claim you—she or I.

ARMANDE

No, I'll not join in making you reveal
So publicly the passion which you feel;
You are, I'm sure, reluctant to confess
Your private feelings under such duress.

CLITANDRE (*to Armande*)

Madam, my heart, unused to sly pretense,
Does not reluct to state its sentiments;
I'm not at all embarrassed, and can proclaim
Wholeheartedly, without reserve or shame,
That she whom I most honor, hold most dear,
And whose devoted slave I am . . .
                    (*Gesturing toward Henriette*)
                                        is here.
Take no offense; you've nothing to resent:
You've made your choice, and so should be content.
Your charms enthralled me once, as many a sigh

13

And warm profession served to testify;
I offered you a love which could not fade,
Yet you disdained the conquest you had made.
Beneath your tyrant gaze, my soul has borne
A hundred bitter slights, and every scorn,
Till, wearying at last of whip and chain,
It hungered for a bondage more humane.
Such have I found, *Madame*, in these fair eyes,

      (Gesturing once more toward Henriette)

Whose kindness I shall ever love and prize:
They have not spurned the man you cast aside,
And, warmed by their regard, my tears have dried.
Now nothing could persuade me to be free
Of this most amiable captivity,
And I entreat you, Madam, do not strive
To cause my former feelings to revive,
Or sway my heart as once you did, for I
Propose to love this lady till I die.

ARMANDE

Well, Sir! What makes you fancy that one might
Regard you with a jealous appetite?
You're fatuous indeed to harbor such
A thought, and very brash to say as much.

HENRIETTE

Steady now, Sister. Where's that discipline
Of soul which reins one's lower nature in,
And keeps one's temper under firm command?

ARMANDE

And you, dear: are your passions well in hand
When you propose to wed a man without
The leave of those who brought your life about?

14

You owe your parents a complete submission,
And may not love except by their permission;
Your heart is theirs, and you may not bestow it;
To do so would be wicked, and you know it.

HENRIETTE

I'm very grateful to be thus instructed
In how these matters ought to be conducted.
And just to prove to you that I've imbibed
Your teachings, I shall do as you've prescribed:
Clitandre, I should thank you if you went
And gained from my dear parents their consent,
So that, without the risk of wickedness,
I could return the love which you profess.

CLITANDRE

Now that I have your gracious leave, I'll bend
My every effort towards that happy end.

ARMANDE

You look triumphant, Sister, and appear
To think me vexed by what has happened here.

HENRIETTE

By no means, Sister. I well know how you've checked
Your senses with the reins of intellect,
And how no foolish weakness could disturb
A heart so disciplined by wisdom's curb.
I'm far from thinking you upset; indeed,
I know you'll give me the support I need,
Help win my parents to Clitandre's side,
And speed the day when I may be his bride.
Do lend your influence, Sister, to promote—

ARMANDE

What childish teasing, Sister! And how you gloat
At having made a cast-off heart your prize!

HENRIETTE

Cast-off or not, it's one you don't despise.
Had you the chance to get it back from me,
You'd gladly pick it up on bended knee.

ARMANDE

I shall not stoop to answer that. I deem
This whole discussion silly in the extreme.

HENRIETTE

It is indeed, and you do well to end it.
Your self-control is great, and I commend it.

SCENE THREE

HENRIETTE

Your frank avowal left her quite unnerved.

CLITANDRE

Such frankness was no less than she deserved;
Given her haughty airs and foolish pride,
My blunt words were entirely justified.
But now, since you have given me leave, I'll seek
Your father—

HENRIETTE

       It's to Mother you should speak.
My gentle father would say yes, of course,
But his decrees, alas, have little force;
Heaven blessed him with a mild, concessive soul
Which yields in all things to his wife's control.
It's she who rules the house, requiring him
To treat as law her every royal whim.
I wish that you were more disposed to please
My mother, and indulge my Aunt Bélise,
By humoring their fancies, and thereby
Making them view you with a kindly eye.

17

CLITANDRE

My heart's too frank for that; I could not praise,
Even in your sister, such outlandish ways,
And female sages aren't my cup of tea.
A woman should know something, I agree,
Of every subject, but this proud desire
To pose as erudite I can't admire.
I like a woman who, though she may know
The answers, does not always let it show;
Who keeps her studies secret and, in fine,
Though she's enlightened, feels no need to shine
By means of pompous word and rare quotation
And brilliance on the slightest provocation.
I much respect your mother; nonetheless,
I can't encourage her in foolishness,
Agree with everything she says, and laud
Her intellectual hero—who's a fraud.
I loathe her Monsieur Trissotin; how can
She so esteem so ludicrous a man,
And class with men of genius and of vision
A dunce whose works meet always with derision,
A bore whose dreadful books end, one and all,
As wrapping paper in some market stall?

HENRIETTE

All that he writes or speaks I find a bore;
I could agree with all you say, and more;
But since the creature has my mother's ear,
He's someone you should cultivate, I fear.
A lover seeks the good opinion of
All who surround the object of his love,
And, so that no one will oppose his passion,
Treats even the house-dog in a courtly fashion.

18

CLITANDRE

You're right; yet Trissotin, I must admit,
So irks me that there's no controlling it.
I can't, to gain his advocacy, stoop
To praise the works of such a nincompoop.
It was those works which introduced me to him;
Before I ever saw the man, I knew him;
From the vile way he wrote, I saw with ease
What, in the flesh, must be his qualities:
The absolute presumption, the complete
And dauntless nature of his self-conceit,
The calm assurance of superior worth
Which renders him the smuggest man on earth,
So that he stands in awe and hugs himself
Before his volumes ranged upon the shelf,
And would not trade his baseless reputation
For that of any general in the nation.

HENRIETTE

If you could see all that, you've got good eyes.

CLITANDRE

I saw still more; for I could visualize,
By studying his dreadful poetry,
Just what the poet's lineaments must be;
I pictured him so truly that, one day,
Seeing a foppish man in the Palais,
I said, "That's Trissotin, by God!"—and found,
Upon enquiry, that my hunch was sound.

HENRIETTE

What a wild story!

CLITANDRE

Not at all; it's true.
But here's your aunt. If you'll permit me to,
I'll tell her of our hopes, in hopes that she
Will urge your mother to approve of me.

SCENE FOUR

CLITANDRE

Madam, permit a lover's heart to seize
This happy opportunity, if you please,
To tell you of his passion, and reveal—

BÉLISE

Hold, Sir! Don't say too baldly what you feel.
If you belong, Sir, to the ranks of those
Who love me, let your eyes alone disclose
Your sentiments, and do not tell me bluntly
Of coarse desires which only could affront me.
Adore me if you will, but do not show it
In such a way that I'll be forced to know it;
Worship me inwardly, and I shall brook it
If, through your silence, I can overlook it;
But should you dare to speak of it outright,
I'll banish you forever from my sight.

CLITANDRE

My passions, Madam, need cause you no alarms;
It's Henriette who's won me by her charms,
And I entreat your generous soul to aid me
In my design to wed that charming lady.

21

BÉLISE

Ah, what a subtle dodge; you should be proud;
You're very artful, it must be allowed;
In all the novels that I've read, I've never
Encountered any subterfuge so clever.

CLITANDRE

Madam, I meant no witty indirection;
I've spoken truly of my heart's affection.
By Heaven's will, by ties that cannot part,
I'm bound to Henriette with all my heart;
It's Henriette I cherish, as I've said,
And Henriette whom I aspire to wed.
All that I ask of you is that you lend
Your influence to help me gain that end.

BÉLISE

I well divine the hopes which you have stated,
And how the name you've used should be translated.
A clever substitution, Sir; and I
Shall use the selfsame code in my reply:
"Henriette" disdains to wed, and those who burn
For her must hope for nothing in return.

CLITANDRE

Madam, why make things difficult? Why insist
Upon supposing what does not exist?

BÉLISE

Good heavens, Sir, don't stand on ceremony,
Denying what your looks have often shown me.

Let it suffice, Sir, that I am contented
With this oblique approach you have invented,
And that, beneath such decorous disguise,
Your homage is acceptable in my eyes,
Provided that you make no overture
Which is not noble, rarefied, and pure.

CLITANDRE

But—

BÉLISE

    Hush. Farewell. It's time our talk was ended.
I've said, already, more than I intended.

CLITANDRE

You're quite mistaken—

BÉLISE

              I'm blushing, can't you see?
All this has overtaxed my modesty.

CLITANDRE

I'm hanged if I love you, Madam! This is absurd.

BÉLISE

No, no, I mustn't hear another word.
            (*She exits.*)

[*Act One* · *Scene Four*]

CLITANDRE

The devil take her and her addled brain!
What stubborn fancies she can entertain!
Well, I'll turn elsewhere, and shall hope to find
Support from someone with a balanced mind.

SCENE ONE

ARISTE

ARISTE (*to Clitandre, who is making
his exit*)

Yes, yes, I'll urge and plead as best I can, Sir,
Then hasten back to you and bring his answer.
Lovers! How very much they have to say,
And what extreme impatience they display!
Never—

SCENE TWO

CHRYSALE, ARISTE

ARISTE

Ah! God be with you, Brother dear.

CHRYSALE

And you, dear Brother.

ARISTE

D'you know what brings me here?

CHRYSALE

No, but I'll gladly learn of it; do tell.

ARISTE

I think you know Clitandre rather well?

CHRYSALE

Indeed; he calls here almost every day.

ARISTE

And what is your opinion of him, pray?

CHRYSALE

He's a man of honor, breeding, wit, and spirit;
I know few lads of comparable merit.

ARISTE

Well, I am here at his request; I'm glad
To learn that you think highly of the lad.

CHRYSALE

I knew his father well, during my stay
In Rome.

ARISTE

Ah, good.

CHRYSALE

A fine man.

ARISTE

So they say.

CHRYSALE

We were both young then, twenty-eight or so,
And a pair of dashing gallants, I'll have you know.

ARISTE

I'm sure of it.

CHRYSALE

Oh, those dark-eyed Roman maids!
The whole town talked about our escapades,
And weren't the husbands jealous!

ARISTE

Ho! No doubt!
But let me broach the matter I came about.

SCENE THREE

BÉLISE (*entering quietly and listening*),
CHRYSALE, ARISTE

ARISTE

I'm here to speak for young Clitandre, and let
You know of his deep love for Henriette.

CHRYSALE

He loves my daughter?

ARISTE

Yes. Upon my honor,
I've never seen such passion; he dotes upon her.

BÉLISE (*to Ariste*)

No, no; I see what's happened. You're unaware
Of the true character of this affair.

ARISTE

What, Sister?

BÉLISE

Clitandre has misled you, Brother:
The passion which he feels is for another.

ARISTE

Oh, come. He doesn't love Henriette? Then how—

BÉLISE

I'm certain of it.

ARISTE

He said he did, just now.

BÉLISE

Of course.

ARISTE

He sent me here, please understand,
To ask her father for the lady's hand.

BÉLISE

Splendid.

ARISTE

What's more, his ardor is so great
That I'm to urge an early wedding date.

BÉLISE

Oh, how delightful; what obliquity!
We use the name of "Henriette," you see,
As a code word and camouflage concealing
The actual object of his tender feeling.
But I'll consent, now, to enlighten you.

ARISTE

Well, Sister, since you know so much, please do
Tell us with whom his true affections lie.

BÉLISE

You wish to know?

ARISTE

I do.

BÉLISE

It's I.

ARISTE

You?

BÉLISE

I.

ARISTE

Well, Sister!

BÉLISE

What do you mean by *well?* My word,
Why should you look surprised at what you've heard?
My charms are evident, in my frank opinion,
And more than one heart's under their dominion.
Dorante, Damis, Cléonte, Valère—all these
Are proof of my attractive qualities.

ARISTE

These men all love you?

BÉLISE

Yes, with all their might.

ARISTE

They've said so?

BÉLISE

None has been so impolite:
They've worshipped me as one from Heaven above,
And not presumed to breathe a word of love.
Mute signs, however, have managed to impart
The keen devotion of each humble heart.

ARISTE

Damis is almost never seen here. Why?

BÉLISE

His reverence for me has made him shy.

ARISTE

Dorante reviles you in the harshest fashion.

BÉLISE

He's seized, at times, by fits of jealous passion.

ARISTE

Cléonte has lately married; so has Valère.

BÉLISE

That was because I drove them to despair.

ARISTE

Sister, you're prone to fantasies, I fear.

CHRYSALE (*to Bélise*)

Get rid of these chimeras, Sister dear.

BÉLISE

Chimeras! Well! Chimeras, did you say?
I have chimeras! Well, how very gay!
May all your thoughts, dear Brothers, be as clear as
Those which you dared, just now, to call *chimeras!*

SCENE FOUR

CHRYSALE, ARISTE

CHRYSALE

Our sister's mad.

ARISTE

And growing madder daily.
But, once more, let's discuss our business, may we?
Clitandre longs to marry Henriette,
And asks your blessing. What answer shall he get?

CHRYSALE

No need to ask. I readily agree.
His wish does honor to my family.

ARISTE

He has, as you well know, no great amount
Of worldly goods—

CHRYSALE

Ah, gold's of no account:
He's rich in virtue, that most precious ore;
His father and I were bosom friends, what's more.

[*Act Two* · *Scene Four*]

ARISTE

Let's go make certain that your wife concurs.

CHRYSALE

I've given my consent; no need for hers.

ARISTE

True, Brother; still, 'twould do no harm if your
Decision had her strong support, I'm sure.
Let's both go—

CHRYSALE

        Nonsense, that's a needless move;
I'll answer for my wife. She will approve.

ARISTE

But—

CHRYSALE

    No. Enough. I'll deal with her. Don't worry.
The business will be settled in a hurry.

ARISTE

So be it. I'll go consult with Henriette,
And then—

CHRYSALE

        The thing's as good as done; don't fret.
I'll tell my wife about it, without delay.

SCENE FIVE

MARTINE

Ain't that my luck! It's right, what people say—
When you hang a dog, first give him a bad name.
Domestic service! It's a losing game.

CHRYSALE

Well, well, Martine! What's up?

MARTINE

You want to know?

CHRYSALE

Why, yes.

MARTINE

·What's up is, Madam's let me go.

CHRYSALE

She's let you go?

38

MARTINE

Yes, given me the sack.

CHRYSALE

But why? Whatever for?

MARTINE

She says she'll whack
Me black and blue if I don't clear out of here.

CHRYSALE

No, you shall stay; you've served me well, my dear.
My wife's a bit short-tempered at times, and fussy:
But this won't do. I'll—

SCENE SIX

PHILAMINTE, BÉLISE, CHRYSALE, MARTINE

PHILAMINTE (*seeing Martine*)
What! Still here, you hussy!
Be off, you trollop; leave my house this minute,
And mind you never again set foot within it!

CHRYSALE

Gently, now.

PHILAMINTE

No, it's settled.

CHRYSALE

But—

PHILAMINTE

Off with her!

CHRYSALE

What crime has she committed, to incur—

PHILAMINTE

So! You defend the girl!

CHRYSALE

No, that's not so.

PHILAMINTE

Are you taking her side against me?

CHRYSALE

Heavens, no;
I merely asked the nature of her offense.

PHILAMINTE

Would I, without good reason, send her hence?

CHRYSALE

Of course not; but employers should be just—

PHILAMINTE

Enough! I bade her leave, and leave she must.

CHRYSALE

Quite so, quite so. Has anyone denied it?

PHILAMINTE

I won't be contradicted. I can't abide it.

CHRYSALE

Agreed.

[*Act Two · Scene Six*]

PHILAMINTE

If you were a proper husband, you
Would take my side, and share my outrage, too.

CHRYSALE

I do, dear.
(*Turning towards Martine*)
Wench! My wife is right to rid
This house of one who's done the thing you did.

MARTINE

What did I do?

CHRYSALE (*aside*)

Alas, you have me there.

PHILAMINTE

She takes a light view, still, of this affair.

CHRYSALE

What caused your anger? How did all this begin?
Did she break some mirror, or piece of porcelain?

PHILAMINTE

Do you suppose that I'd be angry at her,
And bid her leave, for such a trifling matter?

CHRYSALE (*to Martine*)

What can this mean? (*To Philaminte*) Is the crime, then, very great?

PHILAMINTE

Of course it is. Would I exaggerate?

CHRYSALE

Did she, perhaps, by inadvertence, let
Some vase be stolen, or some china set?

PHILAMINTE

That would be nothing.

CHRYSALE (*to Martine*)

Blast, girl, what can this be?
(*To Philaminte*)
Have you caught the chit in some dishonesty?

PHILAMINTE

Far worse than that.

CHRYSALE

Far worse than that?

PHILAMINTE

Far worse.

CHRYSALE (*to Martine*)

For shame, you strumpet! (*To Philaminte*) Has she been so
perverse—

43

PHILAMINTE

This creature, who for insolence has no peer,
Has, after thirty lessons, shocked my ear
By uttering a low, plebeian word
Which Vaugelas deems unworthy to be heard.

CHRYSALE

Is *that*—?

PHILAMINTE

And she persists in her defiance
Of that which is the basis of all science—
Grammar! which even the mightiest must obey,
And whose pure laws hold princes in their sway.

CHRYSALE

I was sure she'd done the worst thing under the sun.

PHILAMINTE

What! You don't find it monstrous, what she's done?

CHRYSALE

Oh, yes.

PHILAMINTE

I'd love to hear you plead her case!

CHRYSALE

Not I!

BÉLISE

It's true, her speech is a disgrace.
How long we've taught her language and its laws!
Yet still she butchers every phrase or clause.

MARTINE

I'm sure your preachings is all well and good,
But I wouldn't talk your jargon if I could.

PHILAMINTE

She dares describe as jargon a speech that's based
On reason, and good usage, and good taste!

MARTINE

If people get the point, that's speech to me;
Fine words don't have no use that I can see.

PHILAMINTE

Hark! There's a sample of her style again!
"Don't have no!"

BÉLISE

O ineducable brain!
How futile have our efforts been to teach
Your stubborn mind the rules of proper speech!
You've coupled *don't* with *no*. I can't forgive
That pleonasm, that double negative.

MARTINE

Good Lord, Ma'am, I ain't studious like you;
I just talk plain, the way my people do.

45

PHILAMINTE

What ghastly solecisms!

BÉLISE

I could faint!

PHILAMINTE

How the ear shudders at the sound of "ain't"!

BÉLISE (*to Martine*)

With ignorance like yours, one struggles vainly.
"Plain" is an adjective; the adverb's "plainly."
Shall grammar be abused by you forever?

MARTINE

Me abuse Gramma? Or Grampa either? Never!

PHILAMINTE

Dear God!

BÉLISE

What I said was "grammar." You misheard.
I've told you about the origin of the word.

MARTINE

Let it come from Passy, Pontoise, or Chaillot;
It's Greek to me.

BÉLISE

Alas, what *do* you know,
You peasant? It is grammar which lays down
The laws which govern adjective and noun,
And verb, and subject.

MARTINE

Madam, I'd just be lying
If I said I knew those people.

PHILAMINTE

Oh, how trying!

BÉLISE

Girl, those are parts of speech, and we must be
At pains to make those parts of speech agree.

MARTINE

Let them agree or squabble, what does it matter?

PHILAMINTE (*to her sister-in-law*)

Ah, mercy, let's be done with all this chatter!
(*To her husband*)
Sir! Will you bid her go and leave me in peace?

CHRYSALE

Yes, yes. (*Aside*) I must give in to her caprice.
(*To Martine*)
Martine, don't vex her further; you'd best depart.

PHILAMINTE

So, you're afraid to wound her little heart!
The hussy! Must you be so sweet and mild?

CHRYSALE

Of course not. (*Loudly*) Wench, be off!
(*Softly, to Martine*)
Go, go, poor child.

SCENE SEVEN

PHILAMINTE, CHRYSALE, BÉLISE

CHRYSALE

Well, you have had your way, and she is gone;
But I don't think much of the way you've carried on.
The girl is good at what she does, and you've
Dismissed her for a trifle. I don't approve.

PHILAMINTE

Would you have me keep her in my service here
To give incessant anguish to my ear
By constant barbarisms, and the breach
Of every law of reason and good speech,
Patching the mangled discourse which she utters
With coarse expressions from the city's gutters?

BÉLISE

It's true, her talk can drive one out of one's wits.
Each day, she tears dear Vaugelas to bits,
And the least failings of this pet of yours
Are vile cacophonies and non sequiturs.

CHRYSALE

Who cares if she offends some grammar book,
So long as she doesn't offend us as a cook?

If she makes a tasty salad, it seems to me
Her subjects and her verbs need not agree.
Let all her talk be barbarous, if she'll not
Burn up my beef or oversalt the pot.
It's food, not language, that I'm nourished by.
Vaugelas can't teach you how to bake a pie;
Malherbe, Balzac, for all their learnèd rules,
Might, in a kitchen, have been utter fools.

PHILAMINTE

I'm stunned by what you've said, and shocked at seeing
How you, who claim the rank of human being,
Rather than rise on spiritual wings,
Give all your care to base, material things.
This rag, the body—does it matter so?
Should its desires detain us here below?
Should we not soar aloft, and scorn to heed it?

CHRYSALE

My body is myself, and I aim to feed it.
It's a rag, perhaps, but one of which I'm fond.

BÉLISE

Brother, 'twixt flesh and spirit there's a bond;
Yet, as the best minds of the age have stated,
The claims of flesh must be subordinated,
And it must be our chief delight and care
To feast the soul on philosophic fare.

CHRYSALE

I don't know what your soul's been eating of late,
But it's not a balanced diet, at any rate;

You show no womanly solicitude
For—

PHILAMINTE

   "Womanly"! That word is old and crude.
It reeks, in fact, of its antiquity.

BÉLISE

It sounds old-fashioned and absurd to me.

CHRYSALE

See here; I can't contain myself; I mean
To drop the mask for once, and vent my spleen.
The whole world thinks you mad, and I am through—

PHILAMINTE

How's that, Sir?

CHRYSALE (*to Bélise*)

     Sister, I am addressing *you*.
The least mistake in speech you can't forgive,
But how mistakenly you choose to live!
I'm sick of those eternal books you've got;
In my opinion, you should burn the lot,
Save for that Plutarch where I press my collars,
And leave the studious life to clerks and scholars;
And do throw out, if I may be emphatic,
That great long frightful spyglass in the attic,
And all these other gadgets, and do it soon.
Stop trying to see what's happening in the moon
And look what's happening in your household here,
Where everything is upside down and queer.

For a hundred reasons, it's neither meet nor right
That a woman study and be erudite.
To teach her children manners, overlook
The household, train the servants and the cook,
And keep a thrifty budget—these should be
Her only study and philosophy.
Our fathers had a saying which made good sense:
A woman's polished her intelligence
Enough, they said, if she can pass the test
Of telling a pair of breeches from a vest.
Their wives read nothing, yet their lives were good;
Domestic lore was all they understood,
And all their books were needle and thread, with which
They made their daughters' trousseaus, stitch by stitch.
But women scorn such modest arts of late;
They want to scribble and to cogitate;
No mystery is too deep for them to plumb.
Is there a stranger house in Christendom
Than mine, where women are as mad as hatters,
And everything is known except what matters?
They know how Mars, the moon, and Venus turn,
And Saturn, too, that's none of my concern,
And what with all this vain and far-fetched learning,
They don't know if my roast of beef is burning.
My servants, who now aspire to culture, too,
Do anything but what they're paid to do;
Thinking is all this household thinks about,
And reasoning has driven reason out.
One spoils a sauce, while reading the dictionary;
One mumbles verses when I ask for sherry;
Because they ape the follies they've observed
In you, I keep six servants and am not served.
Just one poor wench remained who hadn't caught
The prevalent disease of lofty thought,
And now, since Vaugelas might find her lacking
In grammar, you've blown up and sent her packing.
Sister (I'm speaking to you, as I said before),

These goings-on I censure and deplore.
I'm tired of visits from these pedants versed
In Latin, and that ass Trissotin's the worst.
He's flattered you in many a wretched sonnet;
There's a great swarm of queer bees in his bonnet;
Each time he speaks, one wonders what he's said;
I think, myself, that he's crazy in the head.

PHILAMINTE

Dear God, what brutishness of speech and mind!

BÉLISE

Could particles more grossly be combined,
Or atoms form an aggregate more crass?
And can we be of the same blood? Alas,
I hate myself because we two are kin,
And leave this scene in horror and chagrin.

SCENE EIGHT

PHILAMINTE, CHRYSALE

PHILAMINTE

Have you other shots to fire, or are you through?

CHRYSALE

I? No, no. No more quarreling. That will do.
Let's talk of something else. As we've heard her state,
Your eldest daughter scorns to take a mate.
She's a philosopher—mind you, I'm not complaining;
She's had the finest of maternal training.
But her younger sister's otherwise inclined,
And I've a notion that it's time to find
A match for Henriette—

PHILAMINTE

                    Exactly, and
I'll now inform you of the match I've planned.
That Trissotin whose visits you begrudge,
And whom you so contemptuously judge,
Is, I've decided, the appropriate man.
If you can't recognize his worth, I can.
Let's not discuss it; it's quite unnecessary;
I've thought things through; it's he whom she should marry.

Don't tell her of my choice, however; I choose
To be the first to let her know the news.
That she will listen to reason I have no doubt,
And if you seek to meddle, I'll soon find out.

SCENE NINE

ARISTE, CHRYSALE

ARISTE

Ah, Brother; your wife's just leaving, and it's clear
That you and she have had a conference here.

CHRYSALE

Yes.

ARISTE

Well, shall Clitandre have his Henriette?
Is your wife willing? Can the date be set?

CHRYSALE

Not altogether.

ARISTE

What, she refuses?

CHRYSALE

No.

ARISTE

Is she wavering, then?

CHRYSALE

I wouldn't describe her so.

ARISTE

What, then?

CHRYSALE

There's someone else whom she prefers.

ARISTE

For a son-in-law?

CHRYSALE

Yes.

ARISTE

Who is this choice of hers?

CHRYSALE

Well . . . Trissotin.

ARISTE

What! That ass, that figure of fun—

57

CHRYSALE

Who babbles verse and Latin? Yes, that's the one.

ARISTE

Did you agree to him?

CHRYSALE

I? No; God forbid!

ARISTE

What did you say, then?

CHRYSALE

                Nothing; and what I did
Was wise, I think, for it left me uncommitted.

ARISTE

I see! What strategy! How nimble-witted!
Did you, at least, suggest Clitandre, Brother?

CHRYSALE

No. When I found her partial toward another,
It seemed best not to push things then and there.

ARISTE

Your prudence, truly, is beyond compare!
Aren't you ashamed to be so soft and meek?
How can a man be so absurdly weak

As to yield his wife an absolute dominion
And never dare contest her least opinion?

CHRYSALE

Ah, Brother, that's easy enough for you to say.
You've no idea how noisy quarrels weigh
Upon my heart, which loves tranquillity,
And how my wife's bad temper frightens me.
Her nature's philosophic—or that's her claim,
But her tongue's sharp and savage all the same;
All this uplifting thought has not decreased
Her rancorous behavior in the least.
If I cross her even slightly, she will loose
An eight-day howling tempest of abuse.
There's no escape from her consuming ire;
She's like some frightful dragon spitting fire;
And yet, despite her devilish ways, my fear
Obliges me to call her "pet" and "dear."

ARISTE

For shame. That's nonsense. It's your cowardice
Which lets your wife rule over you like this.
What power she has, your weakness has created;
She only rules because you've abdicated;
She couldn't bully you unless you chose,
Like an ass, to let her lead you by the nose.
Come now: despite your timid nature, can
You not resolve for once to be a man,
And, saying "This is how it's going to be,"
Lay down the law, and make your wife agree?
Shall you sacrifice your Henriette to these
Besotted women and their fantasies,
And take for son-in-law, and *heir*, a fool
Who's turned your house into a Latin school,
A pedant whom your dazzled wife extols

59

As best of wits, most erudite of souls
And peerless fashioner of gallant verse,
And who, in all respects, could not be worse?
Once more I say, for shame: it's ludicrous
To see a husband cringe and cower thus.

CHRYSALE

Yes, you're quite right; I see that I've been wrong.
It's high time, Brother, to be firm and strong,
To take a stand.

ARISTE

Well said.

CHRYSALE

It's base, I know,
To let a woman dominate one so.

ARISTE

Quite right.

CHRYSALE

She's taken advantage of my patience.

ARISTE

She has.

CHRYSALE

And of my peaceful inclinations.

ARISTE

That's true.

CHRYSALE

But, as she'll learn this very day,
My daughter's mine, and I shall have my way
And wed her to a man who pleases me.

ARISTE

Now you're the master, as I'd have you be.

CHRYSALE

Brother, as young Clitandre's spokesman, you
Know where to find him. Send him to me, do.

ARISTE

I'll go this instant.

CHRYSALE

Too long my will's been crossed;
Henceforth I'll be a man, whatever the cost.

SCENE ONE

PHILAMINTE, ARMANDE, BÉLISE,
TRISSOTIN, LÉPINE

PHILAMINTE

Let's all sit down and savor, thought by thought,
The verses which our learnèd guest has brought.

ARMANDE

I burn to see them.

BÉLISE

Yes; our souls are panting.

PHILAMINTE (*to Trissotin*)

All that your mind brings forth, I find enchanting.

ARMANDE

For me, your compositions have no peer.

BÉLISE

Their music is a banquet to my ear.

[*Act Three* · *Scene One*]

PHILAMINTE

Don't tantalize your breathless audience.

ARMANDE

Do hurry—

BÉLISE

And relieve this sweet suspense.

PHILAMINTE

Yield to our urging; give us your epigram.

TRISSOTIN (*to Philaminte*)

Madam, 'tis but an infant; still, I am
In hopes that you may condescend to love it,
Since on your doorstep I was delivered of it.

PHILAMINTE

Knowing its father, I can do no other.

TRISSOTIN

Your kind approval, then, shall be its mother.

BÉLISE

What wit he has!

SCENE TWO

HENRIETTE, PHILAMINTE, ARMANDE,
BÉLISE, TRISSOTIN, LÉPINE

PHILAMINTE (*to Henriette, who has
entered and has turned at once to go*)
Ho! Don't rush off like that.

HENRIETTE

I feared I might disrupt your pleasant chat.

PHILAMINTE

Come here, and pay attention, and you shall share
The joy of hearing something rich and rare.

HENRIETTE

I'm no fit judge of elegance in letters;
I leave such heady pastimes to my betters.

PHILAMINTE

That doesn't matter. Stay, and when we're through
I shall reveal a sweet surprise to you.

TRISSOTIN (*to Henriette*)

What need you know of learning and the arts,
Who know so well the way to charm men's hearts?

67

HENRIETTE

Sir, I know neither; nor is it my ambition—

BÉLISE

Oh, please! Let's hear the infant composition.

PHILAMINTE (*to Lépine*)

Quick, boy, some chairs.
(*Lépine falls down in bringing a chair.*)
Dear God, how loutish! Ought you
To fall like that, considering what we've taught you
Regarding equilibrium and its laws?

BÉLISE

Look what you've done, fool. Surely you see the cause?
It was by wrongly shifting what we call
The center of gravity, that you came to fall.

LÉPINE

I saw that when I hit the floor, alas.

PHILAMINTE (*to Lépine, as he leaves*)

Dolt!

TRISSOTIN

It's a blessing he's not made of glass.

ARMANDE

What wit! It never falters!

68

BÉLISE

Not in the least.
(*All sit down.*)

PHILAMINTE

Now then, do serve us your poetic feast.

TRISSOTIN

For such great hunger as confronts me here,
An eight-line dish would not suffice, I fear.
My epigram's too slight. It would be wiser,
I think, to give you first, as appetizer,
A sonnet which a certain princess found
Subtle in sense, delectable in sound.
I've seasoned it with Attic salt throughout,
And you will find it tasty, I have no doubt.

ARMANDE

How could we not?

PHILAMINTE

Let's listen, with concentration.

BÉLISE (*interrupting Trissotin each time
he starts to read*)

My heart is leaping with anticipation.
I'm mad for poetry, and I love it best
When pregnant thoughts are gallantly expressed.

PHILAMINTE

So long as we talk, our guest can't say a word.

TRISSOTIN

SON—

BÉLISE (*to Henriette*)

Niece, be silent.

ARMANDE

Please! Let the poem be heard.

TRISSOTIN

SONNET TO THE PRINCESS URANIE,
REGARDING HER FEVER

Your prudence, Madam, must have drowsed
When you took in so hot a foe
And let him be so nobly housed,
And feasted and regaled him so.

BÉLISE

A fine first quatrain!

ARMANDE

And the style! How gallant!

PHILAMINTE

For metric flow he has a matchless talent.

ARMANDE

"Your *prudence* must have *drowsed*": a charming touch.

BÉLISE

"So hot a foe" delights me quite as much.

PHILAMINTE

I think that "feasted and regaled" conveys
A sense of richness in so many ways.

BÉLISE

Let's listen to the rest.

TRISSOTIN

    Your prudence, Madam, must have drowsed
    When you took in so hot a foe
    And let him be so nobly housed,
    And feasted and regaled him so.

ARMANDE

"Your prudence must have drowsed"!

BÉLISE

"So hot a foe"!

PHILAMINTE

"Feasted and regaled"!

TRISSOTIN

Say what they may, the wretch must go!
From your rich lodging drive away
This ingrate who, as well you know,
Would make your precious life his prey.

BÉLISE

Oh! Pause a moment, I beg you; one is breathless.

ARMANDE

Let us digest those verses, which are deathless.

PHILAMINTE

There's a rare something in those lines which captures
One's inmost heart, and stirs the soul to raptures.

ARMANDE

"Say what they may, the wretch must go!
From your rich lodging drive away . . ."

How apt that is—"rich lodging." I adore
The wit and freshness of that metaphor!

PHILAMINTE

"Say what they may, the wretch must go!"

That "Say what they may" is greatly to my liking.
I've never encountered any words more striking.

ARMANDE

Nor I. That "Say what they may" bewitches me.

BÉLISE

"Say what they may" is brilliant, I agree.

ARMANDE

Oh, to have said it.

BÉLISE

It's a whole poem in a phrase.

PHILAMINTE

But have you fully grasped what it conveys,
As I have?

ARMANDE and BÉLISE

Oh! Oh!

PHILAMINTE

"Say what they may, the wretch must go"!

That means, if people take the fever's side,
Their pleadings should be scornfully denied.

"Say what they may, the wretch must go,
Say what they may, say what they may"!

There's more in that "Say what they may" than first appears.
Perhaps I am alone in this, my dears,
But I see no limit to what that phrase implies.

BÉLISE

It's true, it means a great deal for its size.

[*Act Three · Scene Two*]

PHILAMINTE (*to Trissotin*)

Sir, when you wrote this charming "Say what they may,"
Did you know your own great genius? Can you say
That you were conscious, then, of all the wit
And wealth of meaning we have found in it?

TRISSOTIN

Ah! Well!

ARMANDE

I'm very fond of "ingrate," too.
It well describes that villain fever, who
Repays his hosts by causing them distress.

PHILAMINTE

In short, the quatrains are a great success.
Do let us have the tercets now, I pray.

ARMANDE

Oh, please, let's once more hear "Say what they may."

TRISSOTIN

Say what they may, the wretch must go!

PHILAMINTE, ARMANDE, and BÉLISE

"Say what they may"!

TRISSOTIN

From your rich lodging drive away . . .

74

PHILAMINTE, ARMANDE, and BÉLISE

"Rich lodging"!

TRISSOTIN

This ingrate who, as well you know . . .

PHILAMINTE, ARMANDE, and BÉLISE

That "ingrate" of a fever!

TRISSOTIN

Would make your precious life his prey.

PHILAMINTE

"Your precious life"!

ARMANDE and BÉLISE

Ah!

TRISSOTIN

What! Shall he mock your rank, and pay
No deference to the blood of kings?

PHILAMINTE, ARMANDE, and BÉLISE

Ah!

TRISSOTIN

Shall he afflict you night and day,
And shall you tolerate such things?

No! To the baths you must repair,
And with your own hands drown him there.

PHILAMINTE

I'm overcome.

BÉLISE

I'm faint.

ARMANDE

I'm ravished, quite.

PHILAMINTE

One feels a thousand tremors of delight.

ARMANDE

"And shall you tolerate such things?"

BÉLISE

"No! To the baths you must repair . . ."

PHILAMINTE

"And with your own hands drown him there."
Drown him, that is to say, in the bath-water.

ARMANDE

Your verse, at each step, gives some glad surprise.

[*Act Three* · *Scene Two*]

BÉLISE

Wherever one turns, fresh wonders greet the eyes.

PHILAMINTE

One treads on beauty, wandering through your lines.

ARMANDE

They're little paths all strewn with eglantines.

TRISSOTIN

You find the poem, then—

PHILAMINTE

              Perfect, and, what's more,
Novel: the like was never done before.

BÉLISE (*to Henriette*)

What, Niece, did not this reading stir your heart?
By saying nothing, you've played a dreary part.

HENRIETTE

We play what parts we're given, here below;
Wishing to be a wit won't make one so.

TRISSOTIN

Perhaps my verses bored her.

[*Act Three* · *Scene Two*]

HENRIETTE

No indeed;
I didn't listen.

PHILAMINTE

The epigram! Please proceed.

TRISSOTIN

CONCERNING A VERMILION COACH, GIVEN
TO A LADY OF HIS ACQUAINTANCE . . .

PHILAMINTE

There's always something striking about his titles.

ARMANDE

They ready us for the wit of his recitals.

TRISSOTIN

Love sells his bonds to me at such a rate . . .

PHILAMINTE, ARMANDE, and BÉLISE

Ah!

TRISSOTIN

I've long since spent the half of my estate;
And when you see this coach, embossed
With heavy gold at such a cost

78

That all the dazzled countryside
Gapes as my Laïs passes in her pride . . .

PHILAMINTE

Listen to that. "My Laïs." How erudite!

BÉLISE

A stunning reference. So exactly right.

TRISSOTIN

And when you see this coach, embossed
With heavy gold at such a cost
That all the dazzled countryside
Gapes as my Laïs passes in her pride,
Know by that vision of vermilion
That what was mine is now *her* million.

ARMANDE

Oh! Oh! I didn't foresee that final twist.

PHILAMINTE

We have no subtler epigrammatist.

BÉLISE

"Know by that vision of vermilion
That what was mine is now *her* million."

The rhyme is clever, and yet not forced: "*ver*milion, *her*
million."

PHILAMINTE

Since first we met, Sir, I have had the highest
Opinion of you; it may be that I'm biased;
But all you write, to my mind, stands alone.

TRISSOTIN (*to Philaminte*)

If you'd but read us something of your own,
One might reciprocate your admiration.

PHILAMINTE

I've no new poems, but it's my expectation
That soon, in some eight chapters, you may see
The plans I've made for our Academy.
Plato, in his *Republic*, did not go
Beyond an abstract outline, as you know,
But what I've shaped in words, I shall not fail
To realize, in most concrete detail.
I'm much offended by the disrespect
Which men display for women's intellect,
And I intend to avenge us, every one,
For all the slighting things which men have done—
Assigning us to cares which stunt our souls,
And banning our pursuit of studious goals.

ARMANDE

It's too insulting to forbid our sex
To ponder any questions more complex
Than whether some lace is pretty, or some brocade,
And whether a skirt or cloak is nicely made.

BÉLISE

It's time we broke our mental chains, and stated
Our high intent to be emancipated.

TRISSOTIN

My deep respect for women none can deny;
Though I may praise a lady's lustrous eye,
I honor, too, the lustre of her mind.

PHILAMINTE

For that, you have the thanks of womankind;
But there are some proud scholars I could mention
To whom we'll prove, despite their condescension,
That women may be learnèd if they please,
And found, like men, their own academies.
Ours, furthermore, shall be more wisely run
Than theirs: we'll roll all disciplines into one,
Uniting letters, in a rich alliance,
With all the tools and theories of science,
And in our thought refusing to be thrall
To any school, but making use of all.

TRISSOTIN

For method, Aristotle suits me well.

PHILAMINTE

But in abstractions, Plato *does* excel.

ARMANDE

The thought of Epicurus is very keen.

BÉLISE

I rather like his atoms, but as between
A vacuum and a field of subtle matter
I find it easier to accept the latter.

81

TRISSOTIN

On magnetism, Descartes supports my notions.

ARMANDE

I love his falling worlds . . .

PHILAMINTE

And whirling motions!

ARMANDE

I can't wait for our conclaves. We shall proclaim
Discoveries, and they shall bring us fame.

TRISSOTIN

Yes, to your keen minds Nature can but yield,
And let her rarest secrets be revealed.

PHILAMINTE

I can already offer one such rarity:
I have seen men in the moon, with perfect clarity.

BÉLISE

I'm not sure I've seen men, but I can say
That I've seen steeples there, as plain as day.

ARMANDE

To master grammar and physics is our intent,
And history, ethics, verse, and government.

PHILAMINTE

Ethics, which thrills me in so many respects,
Was once the passion of great intellects;
But it's the Stoics to whom I'd give the prize;
They knew that only the virtuous can be wise.

ARMANDE

Regarding language, we aim to renovate
Our tongue through laws which soon we'll promulgate.
Each of us has conceived a hatred, based
On outraged reason or offended taste,
For certain nouns and verbs. We've gathered these
Into a list of shared antipathies,
And shall proceed to doom and banish them.
At each of our learned gatherings, we'll condemn
In mordant terms those words which we propose
To purge from usage, whether in verse or prose.

PHILAMINTE

But our academy's noblest plan of action,
A scheme in which I take deep satisfaction,
A glorious project which will earn the praise
Of all discerning minds of future days,
Is to suppress those *syllables* which, though found
In blameless words, may have a shocking sound,
Which naughty punsters utter with a smirk,
Which, age on age, coarse jesters overwork,
And which, by filthy double meanings, vex
The finer feelings of the female sex.

TRISSOTIN

You have most wondrous plans, beyond a doubt!

BÉLISE

You'll see our by-laws, once we've worked them out.

TRISSOTIN

They can't fail to be beautiful and wise.

ARMANDE

By our high standards we shall criticize
Whatever's written, and be severe with it.
We'll show that only we and our friends have wit.
We'll search out faults in everything, while citing
Ourselves alone for pure and flawless writing.

SCENE THREE

LÉPINE, TRISSOTIN, PHILAMINTE, BÉLISE,
ARMANDE, HENRIETTE, VADIUS

LÉPINE (*to Trissotin*)

There's a man outside to see you, Sir; he's wearing
Black, and he has a gentle voice and bearing.

(*All rise.*)

TRISSOTIN

It's that learnèd friend of mine, who's begged me to
Procure for him the honor of meeting you.

PHILAMINTE

Please have him enter; you have our full consent.
                (*Trissotin goes to admit Vadius; Philaminte
                speaks to Armande and Bélise.*)
We must be gracious, and *most* intelligent.
                (*To Henriette, who seeks to leave*)
Whoa, there! I told you plainly, didn't I,
That I wished you to remain with us?

HENRIETTE

                                          But why?

[*Act Three* · *Scene Three*]

PHILAMINTE

Come back, and you shall shortly understand.

TRISSOTIN (*returning with Vadius*)

Behold a man who yearns to kiss your hand.
And in presenting him, I have no fear
That he'll profane this cultured atmosphere:
Among our choicest wits, he quite stands out.

PHILAMINTE

Since you present him, his worth's beyond a doubt.

TRISSOTIN

In classics, he's the greatest of savants,
And knows more Greek than any man in France.

PHILAMINTE (*to Bélise*)

Greek! Sister, our guest knows Greek! How marvelous!

BÉLISE (*to Armande*)

Greek, Niece! Do you hear?

ARMANDE

Yes, Greek! What joy for *us!*

PHILAMINTE

Think of it! Greek! Oh, Sir, for the love of Greek,
Permit us each to kiss you on the cheek.
    (*Vadius kisses them all save Henriette, who refuses.*)

86

HENRIETTE

I don't know Greek, Sir; permit me to decline.

PHILAMINTE

I think Greek books are utterly divine.

VADIUS

In my eagerness to meet you, I fear I've come
Intruding on some grave symposium.
Forgive me, Madam, if I've caused confusion.

PHILAMINTE

Ah, Sir, to bring us Greek is no intrusion.

TRISSOTIN

My friend does wonders, too, in verse and prose,
And might well show us something, if he chose.

VADIUS

The fault of authors is their inclination
To dwell upon their works in conversation,
And whether in parks, or parlors, or at table,
To spout their poems as often as they're able.
How sad to see a writer play the extorter,
Demanding oh's and ah's from every quarter,
And forcing any gathering whatever
To tell him that his labored verse is clever.
I've never embraced the folly of which I speak,
And hold the doctrine of a certain Greek
That men of sense, however well endowed,

Should shun the urge to read their works aloud.
Still, here are some lines, concerning youthful love,
Which I'd be pleased to hear your judgments of.

TRISSOTIN

For verve and beauty, your verses stand alone.

VADIUS

Venus and all the Graces grace your own.

TRISSOTIN

Your choice of words is splendid, and your phrasing.

VADIUS

Your *ethos* and your *pathos* are amazing.

TRISSOTIN

The polished eclogues which you've given us
Surpass both Virgil and Theocritus.

VADIUS

Your odes are noble, gallant, and refined,
And leave your master Horace far behind.

TRISSOTIN

Ah, but your little love songs: what could be sweeter?

VADIUS

As for your well-turned sonnets, none are neater.

TRISSOTIN

Your deft *rondeaux;* are any poems more charming?

VADIUS

Your madrigals—are any more disarming?

TRISSOTIN

Above all, you're a wizard at *ballades.*

VADIUS

At *bouts-rimés*, you always have the odds.

TRISSOTIN

If France would only recognize your merits—

VADIUS

If the age did justice to its finer spirits—

TRISSOTIN

You'd have a gilded coach in which to ride.

VADIUS

Statues of you would rise on every side.
                    (*To Trissotin*)
Hem! Now for my *ballade*. Please comment on it
In the frankest—

[*Act Three · Scene Three*]

TRISSOTIN

          Have you seen a certain sonnet
About the fever of Princess Uranie?

VADIUS

Yes. It was read to me yesterday, at tea.

TRISSOTIN

Do you know who wrote it?

VADIUS

             No, but of this I'm sure:
The sonnet, frankly, is very, very poor.

TRISSOTIN

Oh? Many people have praised it, nonetheless.

VADIUS

That doesn't prevent its being a sorry mess,
And if you've read it, I know you share my view.

TRISSOTIN

Why no, I don't in the least agree with you;
Not many sonnets boast so fine a style.

VADIUS

God grant I never write a thing so vile!

90

TRISSOTIN

It couldn't be better written, I contend;
And I should know, because I wrote it, friend.

VADIUS

You?

TRISSOTIN

I.

VADIUS

Well, how this happened I can't explain.

TRISSOTIN

What happened was that you found my poem inane.

VADIUS

When I heard the sonnet, I must have been distrait;
Or perhaps 'twas read in an unconvincing way.
But let's forget it; this *ballade* of mine—

TRISSOTIN

Ballades, I think, are rather asinine.
The form's old-hat; it has a musty smell.

VADIUS

Still, many people like it very well.

[*Act Three* · *Scene Three*]

TRISSOTIN

That doesn't prevent my finding it dull and flat.

VADIUS

No, but the form is none the worse for that.

TRISSOTIN

The *ballade* is dear to pedants; they adore it.

VADIUS

How curious, then, that you should not be for it.

TRISSOTIN

You see in others your own drab qualities.

(All rise.)

VADIUS

Don't see your own in me, Sir, if you please.

TRISSOTIN

Be off, you jingling dunce! Let's end this session.

VADIUS

You scribbler! You disgrace to the profession!

TRISSOTIN

You poetaster! You shameless plagiarist!

VADIUS

You ink-stained thief!

PHILAMINTE

Oh, gentlemen! Please desist!

TRISSOTIN (*to Vadius*)

Go to the Greeks and Romans, and pay back
The thousand things you've filched from them, you hack.

VADIUS

Go to Parnassus and confess your guilt
For turning Horace into a crazy-quilt.

TRISSOTIN

Think of your book, which caused so little stir.

VADIUS

And you, Sir, think of your bankrupt publisher.

TRISSOTIN

My fame's established; in vain you mock me so.

VADIUS

Do tell. Go look at the *Satires* of Boileau.

TRISSOTIN

Go look at them yourself.

VADIUS

As between us two,
I'm treated there more honorably than you.
He gives me a passing thrust, and links my name
With several authors of no little fame;
But nowhere do his verses leave you in peace;
His witty attacks upon you never cease.

TRISSOTIN

It's therefore I whom he respects the more.
To him, you're one of the crowd, a minor bore;
You're given a single sword-thrust, and are reckoned
Too insignificant to deserve a second.
But me he singles out as a noble foe
Against whom he must strive with blow on blow,
Betraying, by those many strokes, that he
Is never certain of the victory.

VADIUS

My pen will teach you that I'm no poetaster.

TRISSOTIN

And mine will show you, fool, that I'm your master.

VADIUS

I challenge you in verse, prose, Latin, and Greek.

TRISSOTIN

We'll meet at Barbin's bookshop, in a week.

SCENE FOUR

TRISSOTIN, PHILAMINTE, ARMANDE,
BÉLISE, HENRIETTE

TRISSOTIN (*to Philaminte*)

Forgive me if my wrath grew uncontrolled;
I felt an obligation to uphold
Your judgment of that sonnet he maligned.

PHILAMINTE

I'll try to mend your quarrel; never mind.
Let's change the subject. Henriette, come here.
I've long been troubled because you don't appear
At all endowed with wit or intellect;
But I've a remedy, now, for that defect.

HENRIETTE

Don't trouble, Mother; I wish no remedy.
Learnèd discourse is not my cup of tea.
I like to take life easy, and I balk
At trying to be a fount of clever talk.
I've no ambition to be a parlor wit,
And if I'm stupid, I don't mind a bit.
I'd rather speak in a plain and common way
Than rack my brains for brilliant things to say.

PHILAMINTE

I know your shameful tastes, which I decline
To countenance in any child of mine.
Beauty of face is but a transient flower,
A brief adornment, the glory of an hour,
And goes no deeper than the outer skin;
But beauty of mind endures, and lies within.
I've long sought means to cultivate in you
A beauty such as time could not undo,
And plant within your breast a noble yearning
For higher knowledge and the fruits of learning;
And now, at last, I've settled on a plan,
Which is to mate you with a learnèd man—
               (*Gesturing toward Trissotin*)
This gentleman, in short, whom I decree
That you acknowledge as your spouse-to-be.

HENRIETTE

I, Mother?

PHILAMINTE

Yes, you. Stop playing innocent.

BÉLISE (*to Trissotin*)

I understand. Your eyes ask my consent
Before you pledge to her a heart that's mine.
Do so. All claims I willingly resign:
This match will bring you wealth and happiness.

TRISSOTIN (*to Henriette*)

My rapture, Madam, is more than I can express:
The honor which this marriage will confer
Upon me—

96

HENRIETTE

Hold! It's not yet settled, Sir;
Don't rush things.

PHILAMINTE

What a reply! How overweening!
Girl, if you dare . . . Enough, you take my meaning.
(*To Trissotin*)
Just let her be. Her mind will soon be changed.

SCENE FIVE

ARMANDE

What a brilliant match our mother has arranged!
She's found for you a spouse both great and wise.

HENRIETTE

Why don't you take him, if he's such a prize?

ARMANDE

It's you, not I, who are to be his bride.

HENRIETTE

For my elder sister, I'll gladly step aside.

ARMANDE

If I, like you, yearned for the wedded state,
I'd take your offer of so fine a mate.

HENRIETTE

If I, like you, were charmed by pedantry,
I'd think the man a perfect choice for me.

ARMANDE

Our tastes may differ, Sister, but we still
Owe strict obedience to our parents' will;
Whether or not you're fractious and contrary,
You'll wed the man our mother bids you marry. . . .

SCENE SIX

CHRYSALE, ARISTE, CLITANDRE,
HENRIETTE, ARMANDE

CHRYSALE *(to Henriette, presenting
Clitandre)*

Now, Daughter, you shall do as I command.
Take off that glove, and give this man your hand,
And think of him henceforward as the one
I've chosen as your husband and my son.

ARMANDE

In this case, Sister, you're easy to persuade.

HENRIETTE

Sister, our parents' will must be obeyed;
I'll wed the man my father bids me marry.

ARMANDE

Your mother's blessing, too, is necessary.

CHRYSALE

Just what do you mean?

[*Act Three · Scene Six*]

ARMANDE

I much regret to state
That Mother has a rival candidate
For the hand of Henri—

CHRYSALE

Hush, you chatterer!
Go prate about philosophy with her,
And cease to meddle in what is my affair.
Tell her it's settled, and bid her to beware
Of angering me by making any fuss.
Go on, now.

ARISTE

Bràvo! This is miraculous.

CLITANDRE

How fortunate I am! What bliss! What joy!

CHRYSALE (*to Clitandre*)

Come, take her hand, now. After you, my boy;
Conduct her to her room. (*To Ariste*) Ah, Brother, this is
A tonic to me; think of those hugs, those kisses!
It warms my old heart, and reminds me of
My youthful days of gallantry and love.

SCENE ONE

ARMANDE

Oh, no, she didn't waver or delay,
But, with a flourish, hastened to obey.
Almost before he spoke, she had agreed
To do his bidding, and she appeared, indeed,
Moved by defiance toward her mother, rather
Than deference to the wishes of her father.

PHILAMINTE

I soon shall show her to whose government
The laws of reason oblige her to consent,
And whether it's matter or form, body or soul,
Father or mother, who is in control.

ARMANDE

The least they could have done was to consult you;
It's graceless of that young man to insult you
By trying to wed your child without your blessing.

PHILAMINTE

He's not yet won. His looks are prepossessing,
And I approved his paying court to you;

105

But I never liked his manners. He well knew
That writing poetry is a gift of mine,
And yet he never asked to hear a line.

SCENE TWO

CLITANDRE *(entering quietly and listening unseen)*, ARMANDE, PHILAMINTE

ARMANDE

Mother, if I were you, I shouldn't let
That gentleman espouse our Henriette.
Not that I care, of course; I do not speak
As someone moved by prejudice or pique,
Or by a heart which, having been forsaken,
Asks vengeance for the wounds which it has taken.
For what I've suffered, philosophy can give
Full consolation, helping one to live
On a high plane, and treat such things with scorn;
But what he's done to you cannot be borne.
Honor requires that you oppose his suit;
Besides, you'd never come to like the brute.
In all our talks, I cannot recollect
His speaking of you with the least respect.

PHILAMINTE

Young whelp!

ARMANDE

      Despite your work's great reputation,
He icily withheld his approbation.

[*Act Four* · *Scene Two*]

PHILAMINTE

The churl!

ARMANDE

A score of times, I read to him
Your latest poems. He tore them limb from limb.

PHILAMINTE

The beast!

ARMANDE

We quarreled often about your writing.
And you would not believe how harsh, how biting—

CLITANDRE (*to Armande*)

Ah, Madam, a little charity, I pray,
Or a little truthful speaking, anyway.
How have I wronged you? What was the offense
Which makes you seek, by slanderous eloquence,
To rouse against me the distaste and ire
Of those whose good opinion I require?
Speak, Madam, and justify your vicious grudge.
I'll gladly let your mother be our judge.

ARMANDE

Had I the grudge of which I stand accused,
I could defend it, for I've been ill-used.
First love, Sir, is a pure and holy flame
Which makes upon us an eternal claim;

'Twere better to renounce this world, and die,
Than be untrue to such a sacred tie.
Fickleness is a monstrous crime, and in
The moral scale there is no heavier sin.

CLITANDRE

Do you call it fickleness, *Madame*, to do
What your heart's cold disdain has driven me to?
If, by submitting to its cruel laws,
I've wounded you, your own proud heart's the cause.
My love for you was fervent and entire;
For two whole years it burned with constant fire;
My duty, care, and worship did not falter;
I laid my heart's devotion on your altar.
But all my love and service were in vain;
You dashed the hopes I dared to entertain.
If, thus rejected, I made overtures
To someone else, was that my fault, or yours?
Was I inconstant, or was I forced to be?
Did I forsake you, or did you banish me?

ARMANDE

Sir, can you say that I've refused your love
When all I've sought has been to purge it of
Vulgarity, and teach you that refined
And perfect passion which is of the mind?
Can you not learn an ardor which dispenses
Entirely with the commerce of the senses,
Or see how sweetly spirits may be blended
When bodily desires have been transcended?
Alas, your love is carnal, and cannot rise
Above the plane of gross material ties;
The flame of your devotion can't be fed
Except by marriage, and the marriage bed.

109

How strange is such a love! Ah oh, how far
Above such earthliness true lovers are!
In their delights, the body plays no part,
And their clear flames but marry heart to heart,
Rejecting all the rest as low and bestial.
Their fire is pure, unsullied, and celestial.
The sighs they breathe are blameless, and express
No filthy hankerings, no fleshliness.
There's no ulterior goal they hunger for.
They love for love's sake, and for nothing more,
And since the spirit is their only care,
Bodies are things of which they're unaware.

CLITANDRE

Well, *I'm* aware, though you may blush to hear it,
That I have both a body and a spirit;
Nor can I part them to my satisfaction;
I fear I lack the power of abstraction
Whereby such philosophic feats are done,
And so my body and soul must live as one.
There's nothing finer, as you say, than these
Entirely spiritual ecstasies,
These marriages of souls, these sentiments
So purified of any taint of sense;
But such love is, for my taste, too ethereal;
I am, as you've complained, a bit material;
I love with all my being, and I confess
That a whole woman is what I would possess.
Need I be damned for feelings of the kind?
With all respect for your high views, I find
That men in general feel my sort of passion,
That marriage still is pretty much in fashion,
And that it's deemed an honorable estate;
So that my asking you to be my mate,
And share with me that good and sweet condition,
Was scarcely an indecent proposition.

ARMANDE

Ah well, Sir: since you thrust my views aside,
Since your brute instincts must be satisfied,
And since your feelings, to be faithful, must
Be bound by ties of flesh and chains of lust,
I'll force myself, if Mother will consent,
To grant the thing on which you're so intent.

CLITANDRE

It's too late, Madam: another's occupied
Your place; if I now took you as my bride,
I'd wrong a heart which sheltered and consoled me
When, in your pride, you'd treated me so coldly.

PHILAMINTE

Sir, do you dream of my consenting to
This other marriage which you have in view?
Does it not penetrate your mind as yet
That I have other plans for Henriette?

CLITANDRE

Ah, Madam, reconsider, if you please,
And don't expose me thus to mockeries;
Don't put me in the ludicrous position
Of having Trissotin for competition.
What a shabby rival! You couldn't have selected
A wit less honored, a pedant less respected.
We've many pseudo-wits and polished frauds
Whose cleverness the time's bad taste applauds,
But Trissotin fools no one, and indeed
His writings are abhorred by all who read.
Save in this house, his work is never praised,
And I have been repeatedly amazed

To hear you laud some piece of foolishness
Which, had you written it, you would suppress.

PHILAMINTE

That's how you judge him. We feel otherwise
Because we look at him with different eyes.

SCENE THREE

TRISSOTIN (*to Philaminte*)

I bring you, Madam, some startling news I've heard.
Last night, a near-catastrophe occurred:
While we were all asleep, a comet crossed
Our vortex, and the Earth was all but lost;
Had it collided with our world, alas,
We'd have been shattered into bits, like glass.

PHILAMINTE

Let's leave that subject for another time;
This gentleman, I fear, would see no rhyme
Or reason in it; it's ignorance he prizes;
Learning and wit are things which he despises.

CLITANDRE

Kindly permit me, Madam, to restate
Your summary of my views: I only hate
Such wit and learning as twist men's brains awry.
Those things are excellent in themselves, but I
Had rather be an ignorant man, by far,
Than learnèd in the way some people are.

[*Act Four* · *Scene Three*]

TRISSOTIN

Well, as for me, I hold that learning never
Could twist a man in any way whatever.

CLITANDRE

And I assert that learning often breeds
Men who are foolish both in words and deeds.

TRISSOTIN

What a striking paradox!

CLITANDRE

                Though I'm no wit,
I'd have no trouble, I think, in proving it.
If arguments should fail, I'm sure I'd find
That living proofs came readily to mind.

TRISSOTIN

The living proofs you gave might not persuade.

CLITANDRE

I'd not look far before my point was made.

TRISSOTIN

I cannot think, myself, of such a case.

CLITANDRE

I can; indeed, it stares me in the face.

TRISSOTIN

I thought it was by ignorance, and not
By learning, Sir, that great fools were begot.

CLITANDRE

Well, you thought wrongly. It's a well-known rule
That no fool's greater than a learnèd fool.

TRISSOTIN

Our common usage contradicts that claim,
Since "fool" and "ignoramus" mean the same.

CLITANDRE

You think those words synonymous? Oh no, Sir!
You'll find that "fool" and "pedant" are much closer.

TRISSOTIN

"Fool" denotes plain and simple foolishness.

CLITANDRE

"Pedant" denotes the same, in fancy dress.

TRISSOTIN

The quest for knowledge is noble and august.

CLITANDRE

But knowledge, in a pedant, turns to dust.

TRISSOTIN

It's clear that ignorance has great charms for you,
Or else you wouldn't defend it as you do.

CLITANDRE

I came to see the charms of ignorance when
I made the acquaintance of certain learnèd men.

TRISSOTIN

Those certain learnèd men, it may turn out,
Are better than certain folk who strut about.

CLITANDRE

The learnèd men would say so, certainly;
But then, those certain folk might not agree.

PHILAMINTE (*to Clitandre*)

I think, Sir—

CLITANDRE

                    Madam, spare me, please. This rough
Assailant is already fierce enough.
Don't join him, pray, in giving me a beating.
I shall preserve myself, now, by retreating.

ARMANDE

You, with your brutal taunts, were the offender;
'Twas you—

[*Act Four* · *Scene Three*]

CLITANDRE

More reinforcements! I surrender.

PHILAMINTE

Sir, witty repartee is quite all right,
But personal attacks are impolite.

CLITANDRE

Good Lord, he's quite unhurt, as one can tell.
No one in France takes ridicule so well.
For years he's heard men gibe at him, and scoff,
And in his smugness merely laughed it off.

TRISSOTIN

I'm not surprised to hear this gentleman say
The things he's said in this unpleasant fray.
He's at court, and as one might expect,
He shares the court's mistrust of intellect,
And, as a courtier, defends with zest
The ignorance that's in its interest.

CLITANDRE

You're very hard indeed on the poor court,
Which hears each day how people of your sort,
Who deal in intellectual wares, decry it,
Complain that their careers are blighted by it,
Deplore its wretched taste, and blame their own
Unhappy failures on that cause alone.
Permit me, Mister Trissotin, with due
Respect for your great name, to say that you
And all your kind would do well to discuss

117

The court in tones less harsh and querulous;
That the court is not so short of wit and brain
As you and all your scribbling friends maintain;
That all things, there, are viewed with common sense,
That good taste, too, is much in evidence,
And that its knowledge of the world surpasses
The fusty learning of pedantic asses.

TRISSOTIN

It has good taste, you say? If only it had!

CLITANDRE

What makes you say, Sir, that its taste is bad?

TRISSOTIN

What makes me say so? Rasiùs and Baldùs
Do France great honor by what their pens produce,
Yet the court pays these scholars no attention,
And neither of them has received a pension.

CLITANDRE

I now perceive your grievance, and I see
That you've left your own name out, from modesty.
Well, let's not drag it into our debate.
Just tell me: how have your heroes served the State?
What are their writings worth, that they expect
Rewards, and charge the nation with neglect?
Why should they whine, these learnèd friends of yours,
At not receiving gifts and sinecures?
A precious lot they've done for France, indeed!
Their tomes are just what court and country need!
The vanity of such beggars makes me laugh:

Because they're set in type and bound in calf,
They think that they're illustrious citizens;
That the fate of nations hangs upon their pens;
That the least mention of their work should bring
The pensions flocking in on eager wing;
That the whole universe, with one wide stare,
Admires them; that their fame is everywhere,
And that they're wondrous wise because they know
What others said before them, long ago—
Because they've given thirty years of toil
And eyestrain to acquire, by midnight oil,
Some jumbled Latin and some garbled Greek,
And overload their brains with the antique
Obscurities which lie about in books.
These bookworms, with their smug, myopic looks,
Are full of pompous talk and windy unction;
They have no common sense, no useful function,
And could, in short, persuade the human race
To think all wit and learning a disgrace.

PHILAMINTE

You speak most heatedly, and it is clear
What feelings prompt you to be so severe;
Your rival's presence, which seems to irk you greatly—

SCENE FOUR

JULIEN, TRISSOTIN, PHILAMINTE,
CLITANDRE, ARMANDE

JULIEN

The learnèd man who visited you lately,
And whose valet I have the honor to be,
Sends you this note, *Madame*, by way of me.

PHILAMINTE

Whatever the import of this note you bring,
Do learn, my friend, that it's a graceless thing
To interrupt a conversation so,
And that a rightly trained valet would go
To the servants first, and ask them for admission.

JULIEN

Madam, I'll bear in mind your admonition.

PHILAMINTE (*reading*)

"Trissotin boasts, Madam, that he is going to marry your
daughter. Let me warn you that that great thinker is thinking
only of your wealth, and that you would do well to put off
the marriage until you have seen the poem which I am now
composing against him. It is to be a portrait in verse, and I
propose to depict him for you in his true colors. Meanwhile,

I am sending herewith the works of Horace, Virgil, Terence,
and Catullus, in the margins of which I have marked, for
your benefit, all the passages which he has plundered."

Well, well! To thwart the match which I desire,
A troop of enemies has opened fire
Upon this worthy man; but I'll requite
By one swift action their dishonest spite,
And show them all that their combined assault
Has only hastened what they strove to halt.
(To Julien)
Take back those volumes to your master, and
Inform him, so that he'll clearly understand
Precisely how much value I have set
Upon his sage advice, that Henriette
(Pointing to Trissotin)
Shall wed this gentleman, this very night.
(To Clitandre)
Sir, you're a friend of the family. I invite
You most sincerely to remain and see
The contract signed, as shortly it shall be.
Armande, you'll send for the notary, and prepare
Your sister for her part in this affair.

ARMANDE

No need for me to let my sister know;
This gentleman, I'm sure, will quickly go
To tell her all the news, and seek as well
To prompt her saucy spirit to rebel.

PHILAMINTE

We'll see by whom her spirit will be swayed;
It doesn't suit me to be disobeyed.

121

SCENE FIVE

ARMANDE, CLITANDRE

ARMANDE

I'm very sorry for you, Sir; it seems
Things haven't gone according to your schemes.

CLITANDRE

Madam, I mean to do my very best
To lift that weight of sorrow from your breast.

ARMANDE

I fear, Sir, that your hopes are not well-grounded.

CLITANDRE

It may be that your fear will prove ill-founded.

ARMANDE

I hope so.

CLITANDRE

I believe you; nor do I doubt
That you'll do all you can to help me out.

ARMANDE

To serve your cause shall be my sole endeavor.

CLITANDRE

For that, you'll have my gratitude forever.

SCENE SIX

CHRYSALE, ARISTE, HENRIETTE, CLITANDRE

CLITANDRE

I shall be lost unless you help me, Sir:
Your wife's rejected my appeals to her,
And chosen Trissotin for her son-in-law.

CHRYSALE

Damn it, what ails the woman? I never saw
What in this Trissotin could so attract her.

ARISTE

He versifies in Latin, and that's a factor
Which makes him, in her view, the better man.

CLITANDRE

To marry them tonight, Sir, is her plan.

CHRYSALE

Tonight?

CLITANDRE

Tonight.

[*Act Four* · *Scene Six*]

CHRYSALE

Her plan, then, will miscarry.
I promise that, tonight, you two shall marry.

CLITANDRE

She's having a contract drawn by the notary.

CHRYSALE

Well, he shall draw another one for me.

CLITANDRE (*indicating Henriette*)

Armande has orders to inform this lady
Of the wedding match for which she's to be ready.

CHRYSALE

And I inform her that, by my command,
It's you on whom she shall bestow her hand.
This is my house, and I shall make it clear
That I'm the one and only master here.
            (*To Henriette*)
Wait, Daughter; we'll join you when our errand's done.
Come, Brother, follow me; you too, my son.

HENRIETTE (*to Ariste*)

Please keep him in this mood, whatever you do.

ARISTE

I'll do my utmost for your love and you.

SCENE SEVEN

CLITANDRE

Whatever aid our kind allies may lend,
It's your true heart on which my hopes depend.

HENRIETTE

As to my heart, of that you may be sure.

CLITANDRE

If so, my own is happy and secure.

HENRIETTE

I must be strong, so as not to be coerced.

CLITANDRE

Cling to our love, and let them do their worst.

HENRIETTE

I'll do my best to make our cause prevail;
But if my hope of being yours should fail,
And if it seems I'm to be forced to marry,
A convent cell shall be my sanctuary.

CLITANDRE

Heaven grant that you need never give to me
Such painful proof of your fidelity.

SCENE ONE

HENRIETTE, TRISSOTIN

HENRIETTE

It seems to me that we two should confer
About this contemplated marriage, Sir,
Since it's reduced our household to dissension.
Do give my arguments your kind attention.
I know that you expect to realize,
By wedding me, a dowry of some size;
Yet money, which so many men pursue,
Should bore a true philosopher like you,
And your contempt for riches should be shown
In your behavior, not in words alone.

TRISSOTIN

It's not in wealth that your attraction lies:
Your sparkling charms, your soft yet flashing eyes,
Your airs, your graces—it is these in which
My ravished heart perceives you to be rich,
These treasures only which I would possess.

HENRIETTE

I'm honored by the love which you profess,
Although I can't see what I've done to earn it,
And much regret, Sir, that I can't return it.
I have the highest estimation of you,

But there's one reason why I cannot love you.
A heart's devotion cannot be divided,
And it's Clitandre on whom my heart's decided.
I know he lacks your merits, which are great,
That I'm obtuse to choose him for my mate,
That you should please me by your gifts and wit;
I know I'm wrong, but there's no help for it;
Though reason chides me for my want of sense,
My heart clings blindly to its preference.

TRISSOTIN

When I am given your hand and marriage vow,
I'll claim the heart Clitandre possesses now,
And I dare hope that I can then incline
That heart, by sweet persuasions, to be mine.

HENRIETTE

No, no: first love, Sir, is too strong a feeling.
All your persuasions could not prove appealing.
Let me, upon this point, be blunt and plain,
Since nothing I shall say could cause you pain.
The fires of love, which set our hearts aglow,
Aren't kindled by men's merits, as you know.
They're most capricious; when someone takes our eye,
We're often quite unable to say why.
If, Sir, our loves were based on wise selection,
You would have all my heart, all my affection;
But love quite clearly doesn't work that way.
Indulge me in my blindness, then, I pray,
And do not show me, Sir, so little mercy
As to desire that others should coerce me.
What man of honor would care to profit by
A parent's power to make a child comply?
To win a lady's hand by such compulsion,
And not by love, would fill him with revulsion.

[*Act Five* · *Scene One*]

Don't, then, I beg you, urge my mother to make
Me bow to her authority for your sake.
Take back the love you offer, and reserve it
For some fine woman who will more deserve it.

TRISSOTIN

Alas, what you command I cannot do.
I'm powerless to retract my love for you.
How shall I cease to worship you, unless
You cease to dazzle me with loveliness,
To stun my heart with beauty, to enthrall—

HENRIETTE

Oh, come, Sir; no more nonsense. You have all
These Irises and Phyllises whose great
Attractiveness your verses celebrate,
And whom you so adore with so much art—

TRISSOTIN

My mind speaks in those verses, not my heart.
I love those ladies in my poems merely,
While Henriette, alone, I love sincerely.

HENRIETTE

Please, Sir—

TRISSOTIN

If by so speaking I offend,
I fear that my offense will never end.
My ardor, which I've hidden hitherto,
Belongs for all eternity to you;

133

I'll love you till this beating heart has stopped;
And, though you scorn the tactics I adopt,
I can't refuse your mother's aid in gaining
The joy I'm so desirous of obtaining.
If the sweet prize I long for can be won,
And you be mine, I care not how it's done.

HENRIETTE

But don't you see that it's a risky course
To take possession of a heart by force;
That things, quite frankly, can go very ill
When a woman's made to wed against her will,
And that, in her resentment, she won't lack
For means to vex her spouse, and pay him back?

TRISSOTIN

I've no anxiety about such things.
The wise man takes whatever fortune brings.
Transcending vulgar weaknesses, his mind
Looks down unmoved on mishaps of the kind,
Nor does he feel the least distress of soul
Regarding matters not in his control.

HENRIETTE

You fascinate me, Sir; I'm much impressed.
I didn't know philosophy possessed
Such powers, and could teach men to endure
Such tricks of fate without discomfiture.
Your lofty patience ought, Sir, to be tested,
So that its greatness could be manifested;
It calls, Sir, for a wife who'd take delight
In making you display it, day and night;
But since I'm ill-equipped, by temperament,

To prove your virtue to its full extent,
I'll leave that joy to one more qualified,
And let some other woman be your bride.

TRISSOTIN

Well, we shall see. The notary for whom
Your mother sent is in the neighboring room.

SCENE TWO

CHRYSALE, CLITANDRE,
MARTINE, HENRIETTE

CHRYSALE

Ah, Daughter, I'm pleased indeed to find you here.
Prepare to show obedience now, my dear,
By doing as your father bids you do.
I'm going to teach your mother a thing or two;
And, first of all, as you can see, I mean
To thwart her will and reinstate Martine.

HENRIETTE

I much admire the stands which you have taken.
Hold to them, Father; don't let yourself be shaken.
Be careful lest your kindly disposition
Induce you to abandon your position;
Cling to your resolutions, I entreat you,
And don't let Mother's stubbornness defeat you.

CHRYSALE

What! So you take me for a booby, eh?

HENRIETTE

Heavens, no!

136

CHRYSALE

Am I a milksop, would you say?

HENRIETTE

I'd not say that.

CHRYSALE

Do you think I lack the sense
To stand up firmly for my sentiments?

HENRIETTE

No, Father.

CHRYSALE

Have I too little brain and spirit
To run my own house? If so, let me hear it.

HENRIETTE

No, no.

CHRYSALE

Am I the sort, do you suppose,
Who'd let a woman lead him by the nose?

HENRIETTE

Of course not.

CHRYSALE

Well then, what were you implying?
Your doubts of me were scarcely gratifying.

HENRIETTE

I didn't mean to offend you, Heaven knows.

CHRYSALE

Under this roof, my girl, what I say goes.

HENRIETTE

True, Father.

CHRYSALE

No one but me has any right
To govern in this house.

HENRIETTE

Yes, Father; quite.

CHRYSALE

This is my family, and I'm sole head.

HENRIETTE

That's so.

CHRYSALE

I'll name the man my child shall wed.

HENRIETTE

Agreed!

CHRYSALE

By Heaven's laws, I rule your fate.

HENRIETTE

Who questions that?

CHRYSALE

          And I'll soon demonstrate
That, in your marriage, your mother has no voice,
And that you must accept your father's choice.

HENRIETTE

Ah, Father, that's my dearest wish. I pray you,
Crown my desires by making me obey you.

CHRYSALE

If my contentious wife should dare to take—

CLITANDRE

She's coming, with the notary in her wake.

CHRYSALE

Stand by me, all of you.

MARTINE

Trust me, Sir. I'm here
To back you up, if need be. Never fear.

SCENE THREE

PHILAMINTE, BÉLISE, ARMANDE, TRISSOTIN,
THE NOTARY, CHRYSALE, CLITANDRE,
HENRIETTE, MARTINE

PHILAMINTE *(to the Notary)*

Can't you dispense with jargon, Sir, and write
Our contract in a style that's more polite?

THE NOTARY

Our style is excellent, Madam; I'd be absurd
Were I to modify a single word.

PHILAMINTE

Such barbarism, in the heart of France!
Can't you at least, for learning's sake, enhance
The document by putting the dowry down
In talent and drachma, rather than franc and crown?
And do use ides and calends for the date.

THE NOTARY

If I did, Madam, what you advocate,
I should invite professional ostracism.

PHILAMINTE

It's useless to contend with barbarism.
Come on, Sir; there's a writing table here.

[*Act Five* · *Scene Three*]

(*Noticing Martine*)
Ah! Impudent girl, how dare you reappear?
Why have you brought her back, Sir? Tell me why.

CHRYSALE

I'll tell you that at leisure, by and by.
First, there's another matter to decide.

THE NOTARY

Let us proceed with the contract. Where's the bride?

PHILAMINTE

I'm giving away my younger daughter.

THE NOTARY

I see.

CHRYSALE

Yes. Henriette's her name, Sir. This is she.

THE NOTARY

Good. And the bridegroom?

PHILAMINTE (*indicating Trissotin*)

This is the man I choose.

CHRYSALE (*indicating Clitandre*)

And I, for my part, have a bit of news:
This is the man she'll marry.

THE NOTARY

      Two grooms? The law
Regards that as excessive.

PHILAMINTE

    Don't hem and haw;
Just write down Trissotin, and your task is done.

CHRYSALE

Write down Clitandre; he's to be my son.

THE NOTARY

Kindly consult together, and agree
On a single person as the groom-to-be.

PHILAMINTE

No, no, Sir, do as I have indicated.

CHRYSALE

Come, come, put down the name that I have stated.

THE NOTARY

First tell me by whose orders I should abide.

PHILAMINTE (*to Chrysale*)

What's this, Sir? Shall my wishes be defied?

[*Act Five · Scene Three*]

CHRYSALE

I won't stand by and let this fellow take
My daughter's hand just for my money's sake.

PHILAMINTE

A lot your money matters to him! Indeed!
How dare you charge a learnèd man with greed?

CHRYSALE

Clitandre shall marry her, as I said before.

PHILAMINTE (*pointing to Trissotin*)

This is the man I've chosen. I'll hear no more.
The matter's settled, do you understand?

CHRYSALE

My! For a woman, you have a heavy hand.

MARTINE

It just ain't right for the wife to run the shop.
The man, I say, should always be on top.

CHRYSALE

Well said.

MARTINE

Though I'm sacked ten times for saying so,
It's cocks, not hens, should be the ones to crow.

144

CHRYSALE

Correct.

MARTINE

When a man's wife wears the breeches, folks
Snicker about him, and make nasty jokes.

CHRYSALE

That's true.

MARTINE

If I had a husband, I wouldn't wish
For him to be all meek and womanish;
No, no, he'd be the captain of the ship,
And if I happened to give him any lip,
Or crossed him, he'd be right to slap my face
A time or two, to put me in my place.

CHRYSALE

Sound thinking.

MARTINE

The master's heart is rightly set
On finding a proper man for Henriette.

CHRYSALE

Yes.

MARTINE

Well then, here's Clitandre. Why deny
The girl a fine young chap like him? And why
Give her a learnèd fool who prates and drones?
She needs a husband, not some bag of bones
Who'll teach her Greek, and be her Latin tutor.
This Trissotin, I tell you, just don't suit her.

CHRYSALE

Right.

PHILAMINTE

We must let her chatter until she's through.

MARTINE

Talk, talk, is all these pedants know how to do.
If I ever took a husband, I've always said,
It wouldn't be no learnèd man I'd wed.
Wit's not the thing you need around the house,
And it's no joy to have a bookish spouse.
When I get married, you can bet your life
My man will study nothing but his wife;
He'll have no other book to read but me,
And won't—so please you, Ma'am—know A from B.

PHILAMINTE

Has your spokesman finished? And have I not politely
Listened to all her speeches?

CHRYSALE

The girl spoke rightly.

146

PHILAMINTE

Well then, to end all squabbling and delay,
Things now shall go exactly as I say.
                    (*Indicating Trissotin*)
Henriette shall wed this man at once, d'you hear?
Don't answer back; don't dare to interfere;
And if you've told Clitandre that he may wed
One of your daughters, give him Armande instead.

CHRYSALE

Well! . . . There's one way to settle this argument.
                    (*To Henriette and Clitandre*)
What do you think of that? Will you consent?

HENRIETTE

Oh, Father!

CLITANDRE

    Oh, Sir!

BÉLISE

                There's yet another bride
By whom he might be yet more satisfied;
But that can't be; the love we share is far
Higher and purer than the morning star;
Our bonds are solely of the intellect,
And all extended substance we reject.

SCENE FOUR

ARISTE, CHRYSALE, PHILAMINTE, BÉLISE,
HENRIETTE, ARMANDE, TRISSOTIN,
THE NOTARY, CLITANDRE, MARTINE

ARISTE

I hate to interrupt this happy affair
By bringing you the tidings which I bear.
You can't imagine what distress I feel
At the shocking news these letters will reveal.
                    (*To Philaminte*)
This one's from your attorney.
                    (*To Chrysale*)
                              And the other
Is yours; it's from Lyons.

CHRYSALE

                    What news, dear Brother,
Could be so pressing, and distress you so?

ARISTE

There is your letter; read it, and you'll know.

PHILAMINTE (*reading*)

"Madam, I have asked your brother to convey to you this
message, advising you of something which I dared not come

148

and tell you in person. Owing to your great neglect of your
affairs, the magistrate's clerk did not notify me of the
preliminary hearing, and you have irrevocably lost your
lawsuit, which you should in fact have won."

CHRYSALE (*to Philaminte*)

You've lost your case!

PHILAMINTE

My! Don't be shaken so!
I'm not disheartened by this trivial blow.
Do teach your heart to take a nobler stance
And brave, like me, the buffetings of chance.

"This negligence of yours has cost you forty thousand
crowns, for it is that amount, together with the legal ex-
penses, which the court has condemned you to pay."

Condemned! What shocking language! That's a word
Reserved for criminals.

ARISTE

True; your lawyer erred,
And you're entirely right to be offended.
He should say that the court has *recommended*
That you comply with its decree, and pay
Forty thousand and costs without delay.

PHILAMINTE

What's in this other letter?

CHRYSALE (*reading*)

"Sir, my friendship with your brother leads me to take
an interest in all that concerns you. I know that you have

put your money in the hands of Argante and Damon, and
I regret to inform you that they have both, on the same day,
gone into bankruptcy."

Lost! All my money! Every penny of it!

PHILAMINTE

What a shameful outburst, Sir. Come, rise above it!
The wise man doesn't mourn the loss of pelf;
His wealth lies not in things, but in himself.
Let's finish this affair, with no more fuss:
                    (*Pointing to Trissotin*)
His fortune will suffice for all of us.

TRISSOTIN

No, Madam, urge my cause no further. I see
That everyone's against this match and me,
And where I am not wanted, I shan't intrude.

PHILAMINTE

Well! That's a sudden change of attitude.
It follows close on our misfortunes, Sir.

TRISSOTIN

Weary of opposition, I prefer
To bow out gracefully, and to decline
A heart which will not freely yield to mine.

PHILAMINTE

I see now what you are, Sir. I perceive
What, till this moment, I would not believe.

TRISSOTIN

See what you like; I do not care one whit
What you perceive, or what you think of it.
I've too much self-respect to tolerate
The rude rebuffs I've suffered here of late:
Men of my worth should not be treated so:
Thus slighted, I shall make my bow, and go.
                    (*He leaves.*)

PHILAMINTE

What a low-natured, mercenary beast!
He isn't philosophic in the least!

CLITANDRE

Madam, I'm no philosopher; but still
I beg to share your fortunes, good or ill,
And dare to offer, together with my hand,
The little wealth I happen to command.

PHILAMINTE

This generous gesture, Sir, I much admire,
And you deserve to have your heart's desire.
I grant your suit, Sir. Henriette and you—

HENRIETTE

No, Mother, I've changed my mind. Forgive me, do,
If once more I oppose your plans for me.

CLITANDRE

What! Will you cheat me of felicity,
Now that the rest have yielded, one and all?

[*Act Five* · *Scene Four*]

HENRIETTE

I know, Clitandre, that your wealth is small.
I wished to marry you so long as I
Might realize my sweetest hopes thereby,
And at the same time mend your circumstances.
But after this great blow to our finances,
I love you far too deeply to impose
On you the burden of our present woes.

CLITANDRE

I welcome any fate which you will share,
And any fate, without you, I couldn't bear.

HENRIETTE

So speaks the reckless heart of love; but let's
Be prudent, Sir, and thus avoid regrets.
Nothing so strains the bond of man and wife
As lacking the necessities of life,
And in the end, such dull and mean vexations
Can lead to quarrels and recriminations.

ARISTE (*to Henriette*)

Is there any reason, save the one you've cited,
Why you and Clitandre shouldn't be united?

HENRIETTE

But for that cause, I never would say no;
I must refuse because I love him so.

ARISTE

Then let the bells ring out for him and you.
The bad news which I brought was all untrue.

'Twas but a stratagem which I devised
In hopes to see your wishes realized
And undeceive my sister, showing her
The baseness of her pet philosopher.

CHRYSALE

Now, Heaven be praised for that!

PHILAMINTE

       I'm overjoyed
To think how that false wretch will be annoyed,
And how the rich festivities of this
Glad marriage will torment his avarice.

CHRYSALE (*to Clitandre*)

Well, Son, our firmness has achieved success.

ARMANDE (*to Philaminte*)
Shall you sacrifice me to their happiness?

PHILAMINTE

Daughter, your sacrifice will not be hard.
Philosophy will help you to regard
Their wedded joys with equanimity.

BÉLISE

Let him be careful lest his love for me
Drive him, in desperation, to consent
To a rash marriage of which he will repent.

[*Act Five · Scene Four*]

CHRYSALE (*to the Notary*)

Come, come, Sir, it is time your task was through;
Draw up the contract just as I told you to.

154